European integration and American federalism: a comparative perspective

European Integration and American Federalism: A Comparative Perspective

Edited by
RICHARD HERR and STEVEN WEBER

Portuguese Studies Program and
International and Area Studies

University of California, Berkeley

Library of Congress Cataloging-in-Publication Data

European integration and American federalism : a comparative perspective / edited by Richard Herr and Steven Weber.
    p. cm.
    Based on a conference held by the International and Area Studies and the Portuguese Studies Program of the University of California, Berkeley, on 6–7 Nov. 1995.
    Includes bibliographical references.
    ISBN 0-87725-182-7
    1. Europe—Economic integration—Congresses. 2. European Union—Congresses. 3. Federal government—Congresses. I. Herr, Richard. II. Weber, Steve, 1961– . III. University of California, Berkeley. Portuguese Studies Program. IV. University of California, Berkeley. International and Area Studies.
HC241.E813 1996
337.1'4—DC20   96-34136
                                                                             CIP

©1996 by the Regents of the University of California

Contents

Acknowledgments	vii
Notes on Contributors	ix
European Integration and American Federalism: A Comparative Perspective	
CRAIG PARSONS	1
The Relevance of American Federalism to the European Union: From Confederation to Federal Union to Nation-State	
RICHARD M. ABRAMS	14
Cultural Policy and the European Union: Toward a Genuine Balance between Common Legacy and Diversity?	
GRETCHEN REYDAMS-SCHILS	19
The European Union between Federalism and Regulation	
JAMES A. CAPORASO	34
Interlocking Politics and the European Union	
THOMAS RISSE-KAPPEN	42
Solving Maastricht's Fiscal Problem	
BARRY EICHENGREEN, JÜRGEN VON HAGEN, and IAN HARDEN	61

Economic Cohesion in an Enlarged European Union

    MANUEL PORTO   69

Some Reflections on the Problem of Differentiation:
The Case of Portugal

    PAULO DE PITTA E CUNHA   85

Agriculture and the Trade Policy Challenges Facing the
European Union

    TIMOTHY JOSLING   90

Institutional Change and the Agenda for the 1996
Intergovernmental Conference

    FRANCIS JACOBS   101

Acknowledgments

This volume is based on the proceedings of the conference on European Integration and American Federalism: A Comparative Perspective, held 6 and 7 November 1995 at Berkeley. Many people and organizations made possible the conference and the publication of this volume. The Portuguese Studies Program (PSP) of the University of California, Berkeley, sponsored the conference, and Professor Steven Weber, Political Science, Berkeley, organized it with the cooperation of Professor Fausto Quadros, Faculty of Law, University of Lisbon. Clara Landeiro, then coordinator of PSP, administered the organization of the conference. Craig Parsons acted as its rapporteur and has analyzed the information and arguments presented there in the introductory chapter to this volume. The Luso-American Development Foundation, Lisbon, and International and Area Studies (IAS), University of California, Berkeley, and PSP provided the necessary funding.

The IAS Publications Program, through the good offices of David Szanton, executive director of IAS, carried out the publication of the volume. Carolina Ressano-Garcia, coordinator of PSP, corresponded with the authors and assembled the papers. The volume benefits from the careful supervision of Bojana Ristich, senior editor of IAS Publications, and the typesetting of Stephen Pitcher.

The editors wish to express our gratitude to all these individuals and institutions. In addition, we owe special thanks to Dr. Rui Machete, president of the Luso-American Development Foundation, and Dean Richard M. Buxbaum of IAS, whose advice and help were essential to the planning and success of the conference.

R. H.

S. W.

Notes on Contributors

RICHARD HERR is Professor of History Emeritus and Chair of the Portuguese Studies Program at the University of California, Berkeley.

STEVEN WEBER is Professor of Political Science at the University of California, Berkeley.

RICHARD M. ABRAMS is Professor of History and Director of the Political Economy of Industrial Societies Program at the University of California, Berkeley.

JAMES CAPORASO is Professor of Political Science at the University of Washington.

BARRY EICHENGREEN is John L. Simpson Professor of Economics and Political Science at the University of California, Berkeley.

JÜRGEN VON HAGEN is Professor of Economics at the University of Mannheim.

IAN HARDEN is Professor of Law at the University of Sheffield.

FRANCIS JACOBS is Principal Administrator for the Committee on Institutional Affairs of the European Parliament.

TIMOTHY JOSLING is Professor of Economics, Food Research Institute, and Senior Fellow, Institute for International Studies, at Stanford University.

CRAIG PARSONS is a graduate student in political science at the University of California, Berkeley.

Notes on Contributors

PAULO PITTA E CUNHA is Professor of Law at the University of Lisbon.

MANUEL PORTO is Professor of Economics in the Coimbra Law School and member of the European Parliament.

GRETCHEN REYDAMS-SCHILS is Professor of Political Science at the University of Notre Dame.

THOMAS RISSE-KAPPEN is Professor of Political Science at the University of Konstanz, Germany.

EUROPEAN INTEGRATION AND AMERICAN FEDERALISM: A COMPARATIVE PERSPECTIVE

Craig Parsons

Academics and politicians agree that the European Union (EU) is not anything like a state, or even that it can adequately be described as a federal system. It is nonetheless clear that the EU shares at least two general characteristics with such large federal systems as that of the United States: a distribution of competencies across multiple levels of government, and the inclusion of heterogeneous subunits in a common institutional framework.

This observation was the basis for a two-day conference held by International and Area Studies and the Portuguese Studies Program of the University of California, Berkeley, on 6–7 November 1995 on the Berkeley campus. Major support came also from the Luso-American Development Foundation, Lisbon. The conference was organized into three panels. The first panel, "The European Union and the Politics of Federalism," compared and contrasted the foundation and development of the American and European political systems. While some strong parallels exist historically and organizationally, the uniqueness of European institutions received the greatest emphasis. We see some federal dynamics in Europe, but the tremendous cultural and institutional heterogeneity of the Union's constituent parts make it unlike any national federation.

The second panel was "The European Union and the Economics of Federalism." Again Europe's heterogeneity underscores the difficulties of integrating disparate countries into a federal framework. Even the relatively homogeneous, longstanding European Community members will require internal reform to move to Economic and Monetary Union. Enlargement has and will put tremendous pressure on the most federal of EU programs: agriculture and regional policy.

The final panel, "The Institutional Agenda," addressed the immediate institutional concerns of the Union in light of the political and economic issues. Participants agreed that imminent expansion to the east is both a threat and an opportunity to Europe: simply defending the *acquis communautaire* in an EU of more than twenty members will require large steps forward in integration. To do so successfully, however, participants in the 1996 Intergovernmental Conference will have to innovate to improve the efficiency, democracy, transparency, and international balance of EU institutions.

A set of questions guided the conference: How can the European Union create sustainable and effective political order over most of a continent while respecting the tremendous diversity of its members? What lessons does the history of American federalism offer for Europe's attempts to do so? How is today's Europe similar to other, more familiar political systems, and how exactly is it different?

THE EUROPEAN UNION AND THE POLITICS OF FEDERALISM

The conference began with an historical comparison of the foundation of the United States and the European Community by Berkeley history professor Richard Abrams. Each union, he noted, was initially drawn together by a common enemy; faced problems of political and economic instability upon "defeat" of that enemy which propelled the union forward (in the European case, only in 1989); confronted difficulties of incorporating unequal members on acceptable institutional terms; and was divided between northern and southern traditions. Furthermore, both the American and European founding fathers were conscious of creating a profoundly new kind of political system. The United States was designed to effect a complete reversal of the classical purpose of the state—i.e., prioritizing the duties of the state to the citizen rather than the reverse. The founders of the European Community sought institutional mechanisms to replace the vicious nationalist cycle of war with a virtuous cycle of prosperity.

The fact that neither group of visionaries could follow clear institutional precedents, however, emphasizes that Europe's story cannot be seen as directly following the American one. Professor

James Caporaso summarized the two unions' contrasts in one observation: the Europeans sought to integrate already constructed nation-states whose political, cultural, and economic differences were far more developed and historically rooted than variations across the American states. Abrams emphasized that cultural and linguistic homogeneity greatly facilitated American integration, and the differences which did exist—between Maryland Catholics and Massachusetts Puritans, for example, or between the northern and southern political economies—were downplayed by a common ideological emphasis on individual opportunity and collective tolerance. America's common culture and ideological base made possible conceptions of union which were never imaginable in Europe: figures as influential as Alexander Hamilton and James Madison considered abolishing the states altogether. Finally, given much greater initial homogeneity than existed in postwar Europe, the American states were better able to create institutions which gradually pulled them into an ever closer union. Of greatest importance for American evolution, argued Professor Abrams, was the early creation of the Supreme Court as the ultimate arbiter of the system. Alongside legal integration, Americans were increasingly united by foreign wars, the outcome of the Civil War, and the rapid development of national-scale markets and industry.

Dr. Gretchen Reydams-Schils's presentation on European cultural policy echoed the conclusion that the U.S.-EU comparison breaks down most clearly in the context of culture. Unlike the United States, the EU exhibits no genuine balance in discourse or policy between common heritage and internal diversity. Cultural policy claims only 0.03 percent of the EU budget and has received real institutional recognition only with Article 128 of the Maastricht Treaty. Furthermore, four aspects of the Maastricht Treaty reemphasized diversity in cultural matters: recognition of the general principle of subsidiarity, permission for subnational representation in Council meetings, creation of a Committee of the Regions, and an explicit prohibition on EU harmonization of cultural policies.

Dr. Reydams-Schils did not view this focus on cultural diversity as misguided but argued simply that there is an overemphasis on diversity relative to the potential "common cultural heritage" component of EU cultural policy. The combination of a focus on diversity with a tiny cultural budget, a "minimalist" view of cultural heritage in economic terms of "goods," and an entangled decision procedure leaves the "Europe" in a "Europe of the Regions" formula extremely weak.

While the European Parliament and the Mediterranean states have pushed for expanded competencies and funds for the EU in cultural policy, even these efforts have emphasized the diversity rather than the commonalities of European cultures. Unless the EU pays more attention to European culture in its own right, warned Reydams-Schils, Europe risks surrendering cultural issues to nationalist, centrifugal forces. This risk may expand in an enlarged EU, producing an unstable mix of increasingly weak nation-states and complex, checkered patterns of cultural diversity.

If the United States and the EU have been built on very different cultural foundations, how do their political institutions compare? Professor Thomas Risse-Kappen assessed the similarities between current EU institutions and the U.S. and German models of federalism. The EU shares features with both national federalisms. U.S. and European institutions display divided federal power, in contrast to the strong German parliamentary government. But Europe resembles Germany in the clear dominance of the executive over legislative institutions, in the broad areas of joint competencies of levels of government, in the relatively large incorporation of nongovernmental actors into decision-making processes, and in an all-pervasive political culture of compromise and consensus. Finally, EU attitudes to territorial inequalities in living standards fall somewhere between American indifference and Germany's strong system of financial redistribution (see below on the economics of federalism).

There appear to be two lessons for the EU: power in federal systems seems to gravitate upward over time, and attempts to slow or reverse this process with strict separation of competencies among levels are difficult to put into practice.* Yet EU analogies are complicated by the fact that the organizational development of the American federation has been most closely paralleled in Europe by developments at the *national* level. As in the United States, a long-developing trend of centralization in European states began to re-

*The German federal system has also undergone a gradual centralization in the postwar period and displays a far greater blurring of competencies (known, when it functions well, as "cooperative federalism") between the *Länder* and Bund levels.

verse in the 1970s; in the last twenty years European states have undergone a general movement toward decentralization. Furthermore, European integration has encouraged these national-level changes; in the European regional policy context, for example, the European Commission has successfully pressed for greater subnational involvement in regional development. In Europe, then, we see a more complex process of national-level decentralization and European-level centralization. The two seem to be mutually reinforcing in the short run, but in the longer term the former may contradict general gravitation of power to the European level, which a U.S.-EU analogy would predict. We are thus left with only one clear parallel to the American case: clear separation of powers among levels of government in the EU is likely to be difficult—if not impossible—to establish and maintain.

This point underscores the analytical weakness and political strength of the concept of "subsidiarity" in recent EU debates. Subsidiarity, as written into the Maastricht Treaty, dictates that all governmental functions should be performed at the lowest effective governmental level. This idea has proven politically popular at all levels of the EU, as it can justify claims for power redistribution in all directions in terms of "objective" functional requirements. Its use can also be politically risky, however, as one participant noted: British government advocates of subsidiarity vis-à-vis Brussels have found themselves confronted by their own language in dealings with Scotland and Wales. In any case, if the development of American federalism is a guide, any application of subsidiarity is unlikely to produce the hoped-for clear distribution of competencies in the EU.

Overall, the first panel's discussants highlighted several clear historical and organizational parallels between today's EU and national models of federalism. There was broad consensus, however, that while specific points of comparison may offer insights—particularly in the organizational relations of multilevel governance—the analogy to national federations does not illuminate the general nature of the EU. The EU does not closely resemble any other state, nor is it obviously in transition to such a state.

How then *can* we describe the EU? Following recent work by Giandomenico Majone, Caporaso defined the EU as an emergent "regulatory state."[1] EU institutions are tremendously weak in the classical extractive, tax and spend functions of the state; the EU budget is less than 1.3 percent of GDP; and the Commission employs only approximately 20,000 people (of whom one-third are translators). Yet no one disputes the influence this "weak" level of government exerts in European societies. By leaving the standard redistributive, stabilizing, and symbolic functions of government to the member-states and by relying on national administrations for implementation of decisions, EU institutions have specialized in "the control and management of international externalities." Despite a tiny revenue base and meager organizational resources, the EU regulatory state can effectively exert influence over political, economic, and social outcomes.

In contrast, it was argued by Risse-Kappen that while Europe parallels some national arrangements, its enormously fragmented central executive cannot be described as anything like a "state" in the Weberian tradition. Although all policy areas have been extensively "Europeanized" in Brussels's complex institutional processes, most organizational power has remained at the national level. Lacking an authoritative Weberian center, the EU is thus best described as a "structure of governance." Rather than displaying hierarchical, "top-down" rationality, EU decision-making exhibits a range of coordinated, "bottom-up" mechanisms.

Another participant took a still less "Euro-statist" view of the EU. Using the Portuguese case to reiterate a point made by Andrew Moravscik in the European integration literature, he portrayed European institutions as clearly strengthening certain national institutions.[2] On the positive side, the separation of the European process from democratic control has allowed national governments to open their economies, and economic integration has delivered a sense of belonging and security to the Portuguese. But rather than improving participation or legal egalitarianism in Portugal's political system, Europe has reinforced the preexisting national-level "democratic deficit" and compounded it with a still greater participatory deficit at the Union level. This increasing separation between governmental processes and citizen participation is normatively untenable. Reform at both European and national levels is necessary to increase the input of both citizens and their direct representatives (national parliaments) into decision-making.

In sum, three themes united the commentaries on the politics of federalism and the EU: history, complexity, and uncertainty. The construction of the EU on the ancient foundations of national cultures and polities has produced an institutional evolution of unprecedented complexity. With that complexity comes uncertainty, ranging from academic uncertainty over the appropriate analogies and descriptions of the EU political system, to political uncertainty over the choice of feasible and desirable steps forward in integration. The EU's challenges to our traditional paradigms and policies demand exactly the kind of reflection promoted by this conference.

THE EUROPEAN UNION AND THE ECONOMICS OF FEDERALISM

Two subjects dominated the panel on the economic requisites and results of Europe's quasi-federal system: the relationship between federal monetary union and national fiscal policies, and the questions of geographical inequalities and fiscal transfers within European regional and agricultural policies.

Professor Barry Eichengreen presented the major challenges to Europe's planned Economic and Monetary Union (EMU) and evaluated the importance of national convergence on numerical fiscal targets. It is now clear that very few of the member-states will meet all of the criteria for economic convergence set as preconditions for EMU in the Maastricht Treaty. Most troublesome for many of the "core" countries—such as the Benelux and even France—are requirements on national spending and debt.* Belgium and the Netherlands will simply be unable to reduce their national debt sufficiently by 1999; for France and several other countries, the debt targets are probably feasible only given flexibility on the other convergence criteria (exchange rates, inflation, interest rates).

Does this mean EMU is impossible? Eichengreen argued instead that ignoring the convergence criteria on national debt would not necessarily undermine a new European currency. In a survey of fourteen federal systems, he found only half had explicit limits on subfederal government spending and borrowing. In the seven federal systems where the federal level collected all major taxes, subfederal spending was limited; elsewhere it was not, as subfederal

*EMU participants are expected to maintain an annual deficit under 3 percent of GDP and a total national debt under 60 percent of GDP.

units could raise taxes and borrow to support their fiscal outlays. Since the EU will clearly be the latter kind of system, with major taxation and borrowing powers remaining at the national levels, there is no abstract need for precise numerical convergence in national fiscal policies. Instead national budgetary procedures should be reformed to include transparent self-limiting of deficits, using institutional devices like the recently created National Debt Board in Belgium.* The creation of budgetary procedures clearly signaling fiscal responsibility to markets is considerably more important than respecting Maastricht's numerical guidelines. Whether such reforms are politically feasible in many countries, Eichengreen admitted, is a separate question.

If federal EMU may not require strict respect of the Maastricht Treaty's numerical criteria, the discussants agreed that the major programs of fiscal transfers in the EU will be forced to undergo substantial change in the coming decade. For the two largest items in the EU budget—the Common Agricultural Policy (CAP) and the Structural Funds of regional development policy—the imminent eastward expansion of the Union poses severe problems. The exacerbated economic heterogeneity of an extended Union will strain current federal-type programs to the breaking point.

Manuel Porto, member of the European Parliament (EP), noted that the Structural Funds are a key part of the European bargain. As the original Community was extended to the west and south, it came to encompass ever greater regional inequalities. In today's EU, disparities in regional GDP per capita vary by as much as a factor of six. The Structural Funds were created in 1975 to address these inequalities. As integration widened and deepened in the 1980s, regional policy quickly became a major priority; the Structural Funds were doubled in 1988 and again in 1993. Porto demonstrated the importance of EU regional policy for Portugal: in recent years, EU programs have provided 15 percent of domestic investment, to which economists have attributed an increase of 0.7 percent in Portugal's annual rate of growth.

Despite these numbers, convergence among the current EU members progresses very slowly. Southern growth will need to sig-

---

*The Debt Board sets limits on the following year's deficit, within which Parliament allocates spending.

nificantly outpace northern growth for many years to redress the imbalance. The North-South fiscal transfers in the Structural Funds, however, are now threatened by eastward expansion. The average GDP per capita of the ten prospective East European members is 11 percent of the EU average, raising the prospect of a wholesale redirection of EU regional policy aid.* Porto emphasized that eastward expansion cannot be pursued at the expense of the Mediterranean member-states: the southern members will accept the challenges of integration only within a redistributive framework. Some system must be designed to preserve fiscal transfers among the current members while extending aid to new entrants. While the discussants were uncertain on exactly how this could happen, Risse-Kappen noted the precedent of German reunification: Germany has "bracketed" its system of transfer payments among the western *Länder*, the *Länderfinanzausgleich*, as a separate policy from investment in the east of the country. However, the East Europeans can expect no parallel to the massive flows of investment from west to east in Germany.

Similar problems await the EU's transfers in agriculture. Professor Timothy Josling presented the Eastern challenge to the CAP in stark numbers: the agricultural production of the ten Eastern applicants is only 7 percent of EU production, but their agricultural population is 130 percent the EU figure. A simple extension of the existing CAP would obviously be prohibitively expensive. Again the solution remains far from clear: the Commission's Agricultural Directorate (DG VI) seems to have moved away from earlier suggestions of two pricing systems, with high subsidized prices in the West separated from a low-priced East by a "Green Wall." Josling argued that such a two-speed system would be enormously divisive, even with a gradual transition to more equal pricing. Instead he proposed that the EU turn this pressure into an opportunity—both within Europe and globally—by tying a major reform of the CAP to a U.S.-EU moratorium on aid to agricultural export. CAP price levels would be reduced, the recent grain and oilseeds reform would be extended to dairy and sugar production, and subsidies would be further decoupled from planting requirements, summing to a general move to direct subsidy payments and competitive prices.

*The ten applicants are Poland, the Czech Republic, Slovakia, Hungary, Slovenia, Romania, Bulgaria, and the Baltic republics (Lithuania, Latvia, and Estonia).

Whether West European governments will be able to seize this opportunity remains to be seen.

In sum, the economic development of the EU, like its political development, is hampered by a heterogeneity without precedent in national political systems. In the greatest imminent step of deepening the EU—via monetary union—disparities among the relatively rich West European states are enough to jeopardize integration. Enlargement to the east will worsen these problems by several orders of magnitude. Yet without exception, the discussants agreed that these challenges can lead to only one kind of response: if only to defend the acquis communautaire for existing members, economic integration will have to continue moving forward. Widening, if it is not to destroy the Union entirely, will require new and innovative steps of deepening.

THE INSTITUTIONAL AGENDA

Both deepening and widening in the 1990s will require restructuring of EU political institutions. In the wake of the Maastricht Treaty and under the shadow of eastward expansion, European leaders are preparing to negotiate new reforms in the 1996 Intergovernmental Conference (IGC). In the final panel, the discussants considered which institutional changes may be seen as necessary and feasible by participants in the IGC.

European Parliament administrator Francis Jacobs structured the debate around the three themes of Commission President Jacques Santer's 1995 Commission agenda: efficiency, transparency, and democracy. To these concerns about the effectiveness of EU decision-making (efficiency) and its accountability to citizens (democracy and transparency), panelists added questions about the balance of national influence in the EU, particularly in terms of large versus small member-states.

First, IGC ideas about improving EU *efficiency* target all four of the central EU institutions. In the Council of Ministers, all members agree that qualified majority voting must be extended in some way in light of enlargement, although national vetoes will clearly be preserved in areas such as the ratification of treaty changes and the EU's "own resources." Less likely to succeed are proposals to reweight certain decisions by a "double majority" reflecting population and suggestions to rework the awkward system of the six-month rotating Council presidency. In the Commission, enlargement raises the possibility of abandoning the principle of at least one commissioner per member-state; this divisive idea may be avoided by designating a smaller central circle of leading commissioners. In the European Parliament, some reallocation of seats will take place, both to accommodate new members without creating a large number of new seats (already at 626) and to redress the overrepresentation of very small countries.* In the European Court of Justice, the principle of representation of each state is likely to be replaced by a system of rotation.† Finally, in the institutional structure more generally, consensus exists on the need to reduce the number of different decision-making procedures (twenty-two by one count) and to simplify the second and third Union "pillars" of home affairs and foreign and security policy.

Second, concerns about *transparency* will probably lead to greater public access to EU documents, a particular concern of the new Scandinavian members. Council meetings are unlikely to be made public, as all agree that this would simply drive meaningful national bargaining out of the public meetings. In an effort to make the EU as a whole more comprehensible to citizens, proposals have been forwarded to rewrite the treaties in a more intelligible way but without substantive changes.

Third, *democratization* of EU institutions will be one of the most heavily debated IGC issues. Increased power for the European Parliament may come through extension of EP/Council legislative "codecision," probably to all areas currently covered by the so-called "cooperation procedure" and elsewhere on a case-by-case basis. The EP (and its national advocates, led by Germany) will also push for a greater role in nominations to top EU posts (the Commission, the future European Central Bank, and the courts), for greater Commission accountability to the Parliament, and for greater EP rights of information and consultation in the extra-Community "pillars."

*Luxembourg's members of the European Parliament represent 60,000 citizens; Germany's represent 800,000.

†The same is true of the European Court of First Instance and the European Court of Auditors.

Outside of the EP, democratic control may be increased through the involvement of national parliaments in EU processes. National parliaments are currently almost completely ignorant of EU developments; with the exception of a few countries (notably Sweden), parliamentarians can access only partial information on major EU decisions post hoc, let alone have opportunities to debate them. Suggestions include allowing national parliaments a set amount of time to debate EU legislation before it is adopted or reinforcing contacts between the EP and national parliaments.

Finally, almost all of these questions touch on the balance of national representation in the Union. One panelist was pessimistic on the consequences of both deepening and expansion for this balance. Most of the proposals forwarded to improve the efficiency of European decision-making—from fewer commissioners, to reallocation of EP seats, to reform of Council presidency rotation, to a decrease in the number of officially recognized languages—will mean less influence for Europe's smaller members. Another panelist maintained that smaller states cannot accept reform of either the current voting weights in the Council (especially the blocking minority) or the principle of the rotating presidency, and that the Commission should be reformed along "one-state-one-commissioner" lines. Francis Jacobs offered an alternative perspective: while it is incontestable that *individual* national influence of the smaller states will decrease with both deepening and widening, there will be *more* small states with greater opportunities for collective action. Both in the Council and the EP, small states may be better able to form effective alliances on matters of common interest.

CONCLUSION

The theoretical and empirical breadth of the discussions makes their brief summation difficult, nor can generalizations do justice to the rich and detailed presentations. With these caveats, the conference led most clearly to the conclusion that comparisons between the EU and the American federation can help us understand specific parts of the EU but are less useful in general description. The two political systems share some fundamental challenges: striking balances of political, economic, and social forces across a large area and multiple layers of government. They display certain similarities in their solutions to these problems, from bicameral representation to the key roles of regulatory and legal integration at the union level. But if many organizational relationships exhibit similar patterns in the two multilayer systems, the vastly greater heterogeneity of Europe's national units undermines broad parallels to the American case. From an analytical perspective, the long historical development of unique national institutions and cultures in Europe cannot be ignored, whatever the current incentives to cooperation and integration. They continue to channel EU development along paths untraveled by the more homogeneous federations which have become nation-states. As the Union expands to the east, these differences will increase, and the possible paths will become still more complex. From a normative standpoint, these differences *should not* be ignored. However admirable the original European goal of replacing nationalist conflict with cooperative prosperity, the progress of European integration must be better justified to its citizens, as a group and in all their diversity.

NOTES

1. See Giandomenico Majone, "The Rise of the Regulatory State in Europe," *West European Politics* 17, 3 (1994): 77–101.

2. Moravscik argues that national executives have been strengthened vis-à-vis both society and other parts of national governments (Andrew Moravscik, "Why the European Community Strengthens the State: Domestic Politics and International Cooperation," presented at APSA, New York, 1–4 September 1994).

THE RELEVANCE OF AMERICAN FEDERALISM TO THE EUROPEAN UNION: FROM CONFEDERATION TO FEDERAL UNION TO NATION-STATE

Richard M. Abrams

It may be expeditious to provide a brief historical background to the subject of "European Integration and American Federalism" by first highlighting points of comparison and then points of contrast between the American and the European experiences. Thus the comparisons:

First, among those with a vision of regional unity, both Americans in the separate states in the eighteenth century and Europeans in their separate states now in the twentieth century confronted the power of self-conscious separateness and the political rewards thereof. Whatever the urgency of their common needs, the thirteen former colonies of Britain thought of themselves as distinct, "sovereign" states, and the local politicos jealously guarded their autonomy, their prerogatives, their power in their own bailiwicks, and their individual bigness in their small ponds.

Second, a common enemy had initially drawn the members of the two unions together—King George's England in the case of the American states, and national insecurity (especially in the face of the Soviet Union during the cold war) in the case of the European Community.

Third, after confederation, after independence from England was won, and comparably for Europe after the cold war was "won," the prospects of and experience with economic distress and the possibility of political instability and internal disorder stimulated a quest for more effective cooperation among the states.

Fourth, when the delegates from the thirteen American states met in Philadelphia in 1787 and (somewhat contrary to their instructions from home) proceeded to devise a constitution to serve "a more perfect Union," they were forced to confront the problem of bringing together on equal terms states that were manifestly unequal in size, population, economic prospects, religious commitments, and social dispositions. The task of the European Union today is similar.

Fifth, when the American delegates met in Philadelphia and devised their constitution, they were conscious of creating, as James Wilson of Pennsylvania stated, "a system hitherto unknown"—what he called "a perfect confederation of independent states."

Actually the constitution that Wilson helped write created something even more truly unknown at the time—namely, a system of government that reversed the timeless historic priorities of the state from those that obligated subjects to serve the purposes of the state to those that obligated the state to serve the purposes of citizens' individual liberty. In that sense, indeed, the American Revolution must be seen as the most profound in modern history—more profound than the French Revolution, which of course took many of its cues from what the Americans were in the process of doing, and surely (as we can plainly see today, more profound than the Russian Revolution of 1917.

What the Philadelphia delegates actually proceeded to do was to turn James Wilson's description, "a perfect confederation of independent states," into an oxymoron—that is, it quickly became evident that any "perfect confederation" or "federation" or union requires a surrender of some substantial measure of independence and absolutist notions of sovereignty. Similarly, any effective European Union requires that the constituent states make comparable concessions.

This completes the points of comparison. As for contrasts:

First, in addition to differences in size, population, economic prospects and conditions, religious commitments, and social dispositions, Europe today faces differences in language plus a far more ancient sense of distinct national identification—not to say often bloody rivalry. This makes the present task of European integration immensely more difficult than what the Americans faced.

Second, many of the Philadelphia delegates who fashioned the American Constitution envisioned a union that substantially superseded the individual states. James Madison of Virginia, for example, went so far as to assert his belief that no fundamental liberties would be lost if the states were abolished altogether. Along with Alexander Hamilton of New York, Madison originally wanted to establish a national legislature with complete power to override state legislatures. That of course turned out to be politically impossible. Even if there were no fear that a strong central government might restore the "tyranny" that Americans believed they had just rebelled against—and indeed there was such fear—the particular, parochial interests of the state and local politicos precluded Madison's wistful wish.

That led to the Great Compromise, which among other things included:

> (a) A bicameral national legislature—i.e., the Congress, which protected the interests of the separate states qua states by providing equal representation for large and small states alike in the upper house (the Senate) and placing the power to ratify or reject major presidential appointments as well as international treaties in that branch of the Congress.
>
> (b) An acknowledgment of the starkest difference among the states—namely, the existence of slavery in nearly half the states—by permitting the slave states to count three-fifths of their slaves for purposes of calculating the number of representatives to which they would be entitled in the lower house of Congress.
>
> (c) A requirement that the President be elected by representatives of the states, the number to which each state was entitled being determined by the number of congressmen it was allotted.

These are just a few of the acknowledgments in the Constitution that the union was one of states, not of citizens of the United States. The Constitution became less an enabling act than a document enumerating the restraints on central government power.

Nonetheless—and this point should be emphasized—there was among the so-called founding fathers, as there appears not to be among today's Europeans, a vision such as that of Madison and Hamilton of a more comprehensively national union, a vision that would gradually find its way into law through legislation and, more important, through judicial decisions. In other words, from the beginning there was among Americans a strong nationalizing force that acted increasingly effectively against the forces of separateness.

Third, provisions in the Constitution prohibited restraints of trade among the states, established a national currency, and required that every state accord full faith and credit to other states' laws, thus creating a free trade zone and an invitation to entrepreneurs to engage in business freely across state lines. Europe is still struggling with the problem. Moreover, it must struggle with it in an industrialized world of segmented labor markets and strikingly diverse political structures designed to cope with the stresses of such segmentation. The comparable difficulties for Americans were mostly (not completely) resolved by the Civil War and the end of slavery 130 years ago.

Fourth, at least equally important was the provision in the Constitution for a supreme court whose decisions were to be recognized by all citizens and the states as the supreme law of the land. It implicitly had the power to define such troublesome and important questions as (a) what constituted "interstate" commerce over which the national government had preemptive power, and (b) the limits of the states' powers to tax and regulate economic activities. Europe has had no such institution. It may be the most crucial of all contrasts.

The Americans moved gradually into the modern era of a relatively unified nation-state. The Civil War and the ensuing constitutional amendments greatly enhanced the power and authority of the national government, although it was more than a quarter of a century later that the change began to take hold.

The industrial, transportation, and communications revolutions forced competing business interests in the United States to seek redress from an increasingly interventionist national government. Although Americans at the creation of the republic had viewed government as the main enemy of liberty, the industrial revolution changed the situation. The rise of the regulatory state, beginning especially during the administrations of Theodore Roosevelt and Woodrow Wilson and reaching a crescendo during Franklin Roosevelt's New Deal, was almost entirely in response to demands from the American business community for government restraints on concentrated power within the private economic sector.

Since 1933 the national government has effectively displaced the states as the locus for most major policy decisions. Agriculture became a nationally managed sector. A wide variety of business decisions, including those pertaining to labor-cost bargaining, came under national review. The national government effectively preempted the most flexible and productive of revenue sources—namely, the income tax—while other taxes, especially payroll taxes for financing the social security system, became a major part of overall tax collections.

By the end of the 1930s, the Supreme Court transformed the interstate commerce clause from a constraint upon national power into an enabling measure that placed nearly all economic behavior within the national government's power to regulate.

In the 1960s and early 1970s a combination of Supreme Court decisions, congressional acts, and executive orders of the President placed additional areas of American life under national control that until then had been left to the individual states to determine: racial relations; criminal court procedures; the conduct of elections and the apportionment of election districts within the states; provisions for safety and health in the workplace, among consumer goods, and in the environment generally; and in widening the boundaries of legally protected alternative lifestyles.

With regard especially to the last, it may be ironic that whereas the original framers of the American Constitution and the American nation feared that a strong national government would endanger individual liberty, American history in the twentieth century has witnessed the contrary: it has been the growth of the national government that has enlarged the boundaries of individual liberties and provided the most effective barriers against violation of human rights. It has been the U.S. Supreme Court along with the office of the President and congressional legislation that have established *national* standards protecting personal privacy, protecting free speech and a free press, governing racial relations, protecting the environment, protecting consumer and workplace safety, guaranteeing a fair trial for those accused of crimes, and overseeing the apportionment of state and congressional election districts to guarantee fair representation. Left to the separate state governments, none of these advances in human rights would have occurred.

It may be our hope that such may lie in Europe's future. But the contrasts between Europe's and the American experience may preclude that outcome. We wait to see.

CULTURAL POLICY AND THE EUROPEAN UNION: TOWARD A GENUINE BALANCE BETWEEN COMMON LEGACY AND DIVERSITY?

Gretchen Reydams-Schils

Should cultural policy be included in a comparison between the European Union (EU) and U.S. federalism? Only 0.02/.03 percent of the EU budget goes to culture specifically (not taking into account the cultural aspects of other policy areas, such as research and education). When we compare this to the more than 50 percent going to agriculture (the "other culture," as a colleague jokingly called it) and the third of the budget for the so-called structural funds, this low figure almost reaches the vanishing point. But if we keep in mind that the total budget of the EU amounts to only some 4 percent of the combined government spending of its member-states, we realize that much of what the EU does has a symbolic function.

In this paper I will present (1) the view from within EU institutions, (2) a critical analysis of the strengths and weaknesses of actual practice, and (3) a larger vision of the potential role of culture in future EU developments.

Like the EU treaty article on culture (Art. 128), the statement of purpose of the U.S. National Endowment for the Humanities (NEH) combines a common element with diversity, and yet the wording in the two texts is significantly different, expressing diverging viewpoints.[1] In the U.S. situation, minority cultures are embedded within a national identity context; in the EU treaty article on culture the common element is phrased as "common cultural heritage"; there is no explicit reference to a European identity and, as we will see below, there is a heavy emphasis on national and regional diversity.

In the heated recent discussion about the future of the NEH and its funding, the government agency received criticism for giving in too much to "identity politics" of minorities and taking away from the sense of national identity.[2] In the case of the EU, on the other hand, it is precisely the common component which is viewed with suspicion, representing the threat of a "melting pot," and the treaty article is predominantly geared toward cultural diversity, at the level of both the member-states and the regions. Cultural policy, then, is an obvious point at which the comparison between the EU and U.S. federalism breaks down, and although it plays a small role in current EU activities, it gives us valuable insights into EU dynamics.

Because much of this paper will be dealing in detail with the treaty article on culture, I include the text here before moving on to the discussion:

> 1. The Community shall contribute to the flowering of cultures of the Member States, while respecting their national and regional diversity and at the same time bringing the common cultural heritage to the fore.
>
> 2. Action by the Community shall be aimed at encouraging cooperation between Member States, and, if necessary, supporting and supplementing their action in the following areas:
> - improvement of the knowledge and dissemination of the culture and history of the European peoples;
> - conservation and safeguarding of cultural heritage of European significance;
> - non-commercial cultural exchanges;
> - artistic and literary creation, including in the audiovisual sector.
>
> 3. The Community and the Member States shall foster cooperation with third countries and the competent international organizations in the sphere of culture, in particular the Council of Europe.
>
> 4. The Community shall take cultural aspects into account in its action under other provisions of this Treaty.
>
> 5. In order to contribute to the achievement of the objectives referred to in this Article, the Council:
> - acting in accordance with the procedure referred to in Article 189b and after consulting the Committee of the Regions, shall

adopt incentive measures, excluding any harmonization of the laws and regulations of the Member States. The Council shall act unanimously throughout the procedures referred to in Article 189b;
- acting unanimously on a proposal from the Commission, shall adopt recommendations.

CULTURAL POLICY AND THE DYNAMICS OF THE EU

In this section I will examine how cultural policy ties in with the evolving competencies of the EU, how it reflects the power distribution among EU institutions, and the differences in the views of the member-states.

Strictly speaking, we can use the term "cultural policy" only for the period after the Treaty of Maastricht, which entered into force in November 1993. Only at this stage did culture get a separate Article under Title IX.[3] Culture is in that sense one of the EU's most recent fields of action (together with education), and its stipulations reveal the same basic structure as those for environmental policy and research and development (R&D), which were added in the Single Act of 1986. However, in another sense culture goes back even to the Treaty of Rome (1957): cultural goods were included under the articles concerning the free movement of goods (Art. 30–36; see below on the Court of Justice). This is important to note because cultural policy within the EU is very much viewed from the economic angle (see below) and seen in terms of "goods."[4] One could argue that what originally constituted a creative way of finding room for the areas of culture and education within very strictly defined Community competencies has now become a limitation and an obstacle to a more conceptual approach.

If cultural action attests to the growing competencies of the EU, it also exemplifies the general principle of subsidiarity (Art. 3b), whereby the EU should not take over what can be done better at the national or subnational level. Paragraph 2 of the treaty article on culture is very explicit in this regard: Community action is to be "aimed at encouraging cooperation between Member States, and, *if necessary*, supporting and supplementing their action." We will look in greater detail at the role of the regions below.

The corollary to subsidiarity is the principle of "added value." The Commission has proven in the past, in its allocation of structural funds, that it has mechanisms for adjusting its course when member-states try to shift their *own* financial responsibilities to the European level. Particularly with cultural policy, the actors involved sometimes express the fear that if more money were to become available within EU programs, this would simply make national states decrease their already overburdened budgets. But subsidiarity, the principle of added value, and the mechanisms of control and adjustment referred to should at least help to prevent this outcome. Additional rules in the game could be negotiated.

We can also ask what one should understand from the phrase that "cultural aspects of other actions are to be taken into account" (par. 4). This could mean several things:

i. Assessing the impact of economic and technological developments and the process of integration itself on culture (but how would that information be distributed and used?);

ii. Identifying economic activities for which there is a clear overlap with culture, in areas such as tourism, with its potential for employment and regional development;

iii. Adding a cultural dimension to already existing actions, such as the research programs (this seems the least likely at the moment; there is no sign as yet that the research agenda of the EU will be moving in this direction; see below).

Let us now take a look at the institutional actors involved in the EU cultural action. In the triangle of Commission, Council, and European Parliament, there is a clear tension between a minimalist approach and a wider vision. Already in April 1992, before the ratification of the Maastricht Treaty, the Commission issued its own communication on future guidelines for cultural policy,[5] in an attempt not only to assure continuity with previously established actions, but also—which of course the text does not spell out—to maintain control of the new developments. To give but one example, according to a Commission official I interviewed, the draft proposal for a cultural heritage program called "Raphaël," which came out in the spring of 1995, was the product of a difficult process (see below).

The European Parliament, on the other hand, is said to have been responsible for the addition of the word "common" to the phrase "common cultural heritage" in the treaty article (par. 1).[6] Big issues can be decided by small words, and if this one word had not been added, there would have been *no reference at all* to any supranational aspect of culture within the EU. (The phrase "cultural heritage of European significance" is more ambiguous.) Through the co-decision procedure, the European Parliament also has gained considerable leverage in the political process previously dominated by the Council.

Not only does the treaty article on culture stipulate a co-decision procedure with the European Parliament, but it also requires that the Council "act *unanimously* on a proposal by the Commission" (par. 5). In another battle of words, "unanimously" was added to the treaty text only immediately prior to the actual Maastricht summit.[7] The combination of the co-decision procedure and a de facto consensus requirement in the Council makes for a very entangled procedure and creates a considerable obstacle for the development of cultural policy. As a Council official explained the dynamics, by the time the Council reaches a consensus, the proposal may be watered down to such an extent that the Parliament refuses to go along, in which case one has to return to the drawing board (which might be exactly what the counter-culture voices within the Council like to see happening). It is true that the same procedural conditions apply to R&D. But because R&D in its current form fits in better with the economic aims of the Community, the strict conditions seem to create fewer problems there—though matters can get complicated and officials can be caught complaining about "a collection of hidden dinosaurs"—than in the area of culture, which is much more controversial. If anything were expected for cultural policy from the 1996 Intergovernmental Conference, it probably would be in a move from unanimity to (qualified) majority voting within the Council.

As a direct result of the Maastricht negotiations, a new organ saw the light: the Committee of the Regions; it should be consulted in matters pertaining to the regions, including culture. This consultative body is still in its beginning stages, and it has a heterogeneous composition because it represents subnational units with varying degrees of independence and power. Much of its effectiveness will also depend on the Council's willingness to take its advice into account. For now it suffices to note that the Committee of the Regions is yet another factor which tips the balance to the diversity side of the debate.

The Court of Justice has historically played an important role in the opening up of the areas of culture and education for Community action; through its rulings it provided loopholes within the given restrictions and economic focus. But will the Court in the future be able to handle the increasing regional participation, and how will it adapt to deal with subnational levels?

The development of the EU's competencies in the area of culture can also inform us about the differences among the member-states and their varying standpoints.

The United Kingdom (UK) can easily be singled out as having an overall "minimalist view" of what the EU should do: it should merely promote a free-market economy through deregulation (and not add a new superstructure of its own). The British of course do not stand alone on this and often are joined by others like the Dutch or the Germans, depending on the issue. But "cultural policy" would certainly qualify as a nonentity for the UK, also because it is a nonentity on the national level. "Cultural policy" might make sense for the French; it does not fit into the political landscape of the UK. So if someone had been using this phrase in the Council, he or she would have lost the day from the very onset of the debate. There is a good reason for the more cumbersome expression "Community action in the field of culture."

Germany is a very interesting case because of its own federal structure and the relationship between the national level and the sixteen *Länder*. Culture belongs to the competencies of the Länder, but until the Maastricht Treaty, only the national Germany was represented in the Council meetings. From 1987 onwards, however, the Länder succeeded in having their voices heard in matters dealing with culture. With the negotiations of Maastricht, they heavily insisted on the subsidiarity principle; pushed, together with Spain and Belgium, for the creation of the Committee of the Regions; and threatened "to do ugly things" if the treaty would not make room for the representation of subnational units at the Council table, which it in fact now does under Article 146. Thus the creation of many safety valves for diversity and the recognition of subnational units received a politically crucial impetus from the Länder. But it remains to be seen how these will work in practice. We have already taken a brief look at the Committee of the Regions. Even though Germany will in all likelihood continue to speak with one voice in the Council meetings because of a mechanism of consensus-building at the Bundesrat level, a rotation among sixteen representatives might create problems.

In the Danish referendum on the Maastricht Treaty, the smaller member-states' (and possibly also regions') fear of the EU's "melting pot" clearly surfaced. It is often said—and used in the media—that EU leveling would leave Europeans with a bland "common denominator" culture. Although the fear concerns more areas than culture, it is acutely felt in this domain and has proven to be a powerful element in political discourse.

France has earned a reputation for being a forerunner in the conflict with the United States over the audiovisual sector, though this matter is not an exclusively French concern. (The conflict, it has to be remembered, made it into the GATT negotiations as well.) Note that the audiovisual sector is the only area explicitly mentioned in the treaty article on culture. The larger issue at stake here is the perceived threat to European/national culture coming from *outside* influences, primarily the United States.

Finally, there are many indications that next to the European Parliament, it is the Mediterranean countries—primarily Greece, Portugal, and Spain—that push cultural policy forward within the EU. The responsibility for culture within the Commission has been given to a Spanish (and previously a Portuguese) commissioner. The Belgian and Greek presidencies of the Council/EU organized the necessary consultative meetings to get the cultural heritage program Raphaël going. (The meetings were held in Belgium, Athens, and Lisbon, in chronological order.)

There could be several explanations for the trend of the Mediterranean countries' influence. But there is certainly more to the issue than simply the fact that soft areas like culture tend to be assigned to newcomers and/or less powerful players in the public sphere (like women). Culture is a serious matter in the Mediterranean, and it also ties in (via tourism) with economics, employment, and regional development. That culture can be identified with "movable goods" is a very sensitive and important issue, notably for the

Greeks, because so much of their cultural heritage has been carried off.

CURRENT EU CULTURAL POLICY

This overview should help us see the main characteristics of EU cultural policy. In what follows, I will draw attention to major gaps in the action as it stands now.

The budget assigned to cultural action is without doubt the most evident weakness. Although it would be difficult to assign a ceiling to spending for culture, we can safely state that currently the gulf is too wide between concepts such as (on the one hand) the "Big Space without Frontiers"—a concept which the Commission used in its own 1992 communication—or the almost poetic language of "contributing to the *flowering*" of cultures and the peanuts budget, on the other hand. If the EU wants to take its newly assigned responsibility seriously, this will require more serious commitments.*

Related to this first issue is the fact that traditionally the Commission has been opting for "high visibility" actions that have tangible results and yield a high public relations return for a minimal effort. The largely symbolic actions such as the "European City of Culture" have to be seen in this light as well. The point is not to deny the value of these initiatives—they might very well be the sensible thing to do under the given circumstances—but to claim there is also a need for a more coherent and deeper approach.

To summarize, I have discussed four aspects of the Maastricht Treaty that give weight to diversity in cultural matters: the general principle of subsidiarity, the presence of subnational representatives at Council meetings, the Committee of the Regions, and the *explicit* harmonization prohibition. (The first three are relevant for other areas of EU policy as well; the last is embedded within the treaty article on culture.) Cultural policy too attests to the development of a multilevel governance system.

*Note that the Commission also tries to promote business sponsorship of the arts through its support of the Comité Européen pour le Rapprochement de l'Economie et de la Culture (CEREC).

The point here is not that the emphasis on cultural diversity is misguided, but that there might be an overemphasis on diversity *compared to* what the EU does with the "common cultural heritage" component. To ignore the importance of subsidiarity, cultural diversity, and regional identity would be to misunderstand fundamentally the dynamics of the EU and the "nature of the beast" (that it indeed defies description in terms of federalism versus intergovernmentalism). It would also be a mistake to consider regional diversity solely as contributing to the danger of fragmentation; interregional alliances that reach across national borders and change the national member-states' sphere of influence can be a powerful tool in enhancing integration.[8] A "Europe of the Regions" is an attractive concept.

If we consider the emphasis on cultural diversity in combination with the limited budget, the entangled decision procedure, and the "minimalist" view of cultural heritage in economic terms of "goods," it should become clear that currently the "Europe" in the formula is very weak—too weak, I would argue, when we are dealing with the cultural policy of the EU. Hence the subtitle of this paper: Toward a *Genuine Balance* between Common Legacy and Diversity.

Can we talk about a European cultural identity in a meaningful manner? (When I raised this question at the conference where this paper was first presented, my U.S. neighbor to one side said, "Europeans tend to overemphasize the differences among their cultures." My European colleague to the other side grumbled, "Which common heritage? There is no such thing!") There are many traps to be avoided. First, selling flags and ballpoints, paying lip service to culture in political speeches with the occasional stereotype line about Christendom and Erasmus (the humanist, not the program; he came first), or promoting a "sex, love, and babies" approach, as Umberto Eco did in a recent newspaper article when referring to the EU student exchange program[9]—all these approaches may be pleasant, but they have their limitations. Culture is not merely a jester at the king's court. (The symbolic actions the EU has been taking—such as designating a European City of Culture on a yearly basis since 1985—while highly visible are also very limited in scope.)

A second mistake would be to expect that the actors in the EU need agree on what constitutes a common cultural component before they can move into action. If we need a specific and detailed consensus, there will be no end to the debate. A more pragmatic approach would see a common culture as a *dynamic and evolving* concept, in which both the material and the intellectual aspects of the European cultural heritage are given attention, and the current identity is the outcome of a dialogue between the European cultures and peoples, a dialogue which does *not* require a harmonization of laws and regulations. Elsewhere I have argued in greater detail that the common cultural heritage is to be found not only in movable and nonmovable goods, but also in an intellectual debate which draws on a common depository of texts.[10]

Third, a cultural policy which wants to include a common approach and combine cooperation among member-states with EU initiatives should not be seen as necessarily creating a melting pot and undermining diversity. Here the concept of multiple identities can bring out the full potential of the "Europe of the Regions" idea: a European culture is not meant to replace locally rooted identities, but to complement them and to add a larger perspective, in the full sense of the word.

Finally, it might be easier to define an identity vis-à-vis an outsider, but a European identity should also not exclusively rely on the mechanism of extended chauvinism, of seeing itself as threatened by (for instance) U.S. culture (even though, realistically speaking, it might be impossible, or even undesirable, to get rid of this kind of tension altogether).

Given the treaty's language about "common cultural heritage" and its encouragement of "improving the knowledge and dissemination of the culture and history of the European peoples," one might naturally expect there to be room not only for the arts and artistic creation, but for the humanities as well. With this expectation comes another one: that the *research* agenda of the EU might in the long run reflect this new emphasis and that the ties among culture, education (with its success story of student exchanges), *and research* be strengthened.

Yet the humanities are hardly in evidence. For these academic disciplines, there was no significant change in setup between the third and fourth research framework programs, though the latter was finished after Maastricht. Between 1990 and 1994 only 6–9 research projects of a total of 173 accepted projects within the group Economy, Social and Human Sciences went to the humanities, and this is largely due to the fact that currently only those projects can be considered which have ties with other components of the research framework itself (a stipulation which did not prevent two projects on Aristotle from being accepted!)

In its 1992 communication on culture the Commission put three items under the heading of "common legacy": (1) cultural heritage, (2) books and reading, and (3) the audiovisual sector. Is it not strange that the EU would spend money on and devote energy to the conservation of library collections and rare books and translations of books, but not invest in the *people* who (in some cases) are the only ones who have the skills to *interpret* those books and (in others) to complement the living dialogue among readers with an academic debate?

It is clear from the spring 1995 Commission proposal for the Raphaël program that the Commission still sees cultural heritage as primarily referring to goods, movable and nonmovable;[11] the areas mentioned explicitly in the preamble are architectural heritage, works of art, artifacts, and archives, though there is also a reference to the changing nature of the definition of heritage. The document focuses on preservation and management of sites/collections; a lot of attention is devoted to mapping existing practices within member-states and regions, professional training, and applications of technology, though research is also mentioned.

In sharp contrast, there are several voices on the European scene now pleading explicitly for a wider interpretation of cultural heritage. The European Science Foundation, an umbrella organization for national academies, research councils, and other institutional supporters of research, tries to use the treaty article on culture, and notably par. 4, to gain access to the EU research agenda for the humanities. The Danish Research Council for the Humanities formed a EURO-group in 1995 that wants to target the 1999 fifth framework program for research, stipulating explicitly that the treaty article on culture "will have implications for Community research programmes," and that "it is necessary to create a new agenda for a European cultural research programme."[12] The proposal includes a plea for the inclusion of both a "*separate* humanistic research programme as a supplement to the socio-economic programme" (which got included in the previous round of negotiations) and a further enhancement of the contributions of the humanities to other aspects of the research agenda.

Clearly these organizations are not on the same wave length as the Commission, however, and given that historically Euratom really is the backbone of the EU's research division, a very long negotiation process might lie ahead in order to reconcile the minimalist interpretation of cultural heritage with larger demands. (That is not even taking into account that the humanities traditions vary greatly from member-state to member-state, but this brings us back to the previous point: an EU approach does *not* require harmonization of national and regional practices.)[13]

CULTURAL POLICY AS A POLITICAL TOOL?

If we return to the statement of the U.S. NEH to which I referred above, we notice that it does not shy away from expressing its mission in political terms: "Democracy demands wisdom and vision in its citizens" (from the National Foundation on the Arts and Humanities Act of 1965). Lest we should think that Europeans are unwilling to make this move, the proposal from the Danish Research Council for the Humanities cited above reads: "A programme for European cultural research is necessary . . . for ethical and democratic solutions in the project for European cooperation." The "citizen of Europe" that made it into the Maastricht Treaty should not have to wear the emperor's new clothes—that is, go naked.

Has the risk of leveling out and harmonizing the cultural diversity within the EU been correctly assessed and located? It is unlikely that the EU's budget for culture will ever be so important as to have a drastic effect, and the harmonization prohibition is a sufficient guarantee that even if the Community becomes more active in this area, it will have to respect national and regional differences. On the other hand, one could argue that it is precisely noninterference in cultural matters, the free-market process, and deregulation that could constitute a real threat to cultural diversity.

If the common component of cultural policy and the question of a European identity is further ignored, the EU could run the risk of fueling centrifugal forces which derive at least part of their strength from nationalist and chauvinistic tendencies, and these forces could put a strain on integration, if not pull it apart. The so-called "Flemish movement" would make a good case study. Already as early as the late 1920s there was a strong tension within this movement between the adherents of a pacifist approach (which would be open to the international community at large) and those who followed a more aggressive, nationalistic line. In the current Belgian political landscape, the Volksunie, which has been an eloquent proponent of a Europe of the Regions, has lost ground not only to the mainstream parties of a more federal Belgium, in which Flanders has now gained a position of relative strength, but also to the ultra-right Vlaams Blok. Are we willing to assess the potential risks of promoting regional diversity, especially in a future enlarged EU, where we could get a combination of increasingly weaker nation-states and highly complex, checkered, and unstable patterns of cultural diversity?

Finally, I would like to take a look at the potential political advantages for the EU of a genuine balance between the common culture component of the treaty article and cultural diversity.

A deeper notion of common identity would underscore the principle of the EU as dealing with a set of democratic rules to which every member-state, no matter how big and how important, would have to conform.[14] (This principle is currently still undermined, though, by a de facto veto mechanism within the Council and by its consensus *modus vivendi*.) More specifically for culture, a common component could similarly keep the predominance of one culture or the alignment of a group of cultures in check. The cultural diversity emphasis, on the other hand, could help underscore the political and economic leverage of smaller countries, a minority group of countries, regions, or even transnational regional alliances.

As the EU moves on to a next crucial stage in its development with the upcoming Intergovernmental Conference, it no doubt will have bigger issues on its mind than cultural policy. But if the analysis of this paper holds, the EU and its actors at the institutional, member-state, and subnational levels could benefit greatly in the long run from a cultural policy consisting of an equilibrium between common goals and diversity, an equilibrium which does not require a full-fledged federalism to yield its fruits after the "flowering."

NOTES

1. In the 1995 "Overview of Endowment Programs" of the NEH, we read, under the heading of "Special Initiative: A National Conversation," the following statement by Sheldon Hackney, chairman: "All of our people—left, right and center—have a responsibility to examine and discuss what unites us as a country, what we share as common American values in a nation composed of many divergent groups and beliefs. For too long, we have let what divides us capture the headlines and sound bites, polarizing us rather than bringing us together. I am proposing a national conversation open to all Americans, a conversation in which all voices are heard, in which we grapple seriously with the meaning of American pluralism."

2. For a flavor of the rhetoric involved, see R. Hughes, "Pulling the Fuse on Culture," *Time*, 7 August 1995, pp. 60–68, and Newt Gingrich's reply in the issue of 21 August 1995, p. 70. I would like to thank Robert P. Burke of the Institute of Scholarship in the Liberal Arts at the University of Notre Dame for keeping me informed about this issue.

3. L. Bekemans and R. Lombaert, "Culture and Institutions: An Introductory Note," in *Culture: Building Stone for Europe 2002*, ed. L. Bekemans, pp. 194–96 (1994), distinguish several phases in the Community actions for culture. See also A. Balodimos and L. Bekemans, *Etude concernant les modifications apportées par le Traité sur l'Union Politique et qui concerne l'éducation, la formation professionelle et la culture* (Luxembourg: Parlement Européen, Direction Générale des Etudes, Dir. A, 1992); reprinted, with revisions and useful annexes of EU documents and bibliography, in *L' Identité européene*, ed. R. Picht, pp. 167–221 (TEPSA study, 1994).

4. One look at the table of contents of A. Loman et al., *Culture and Community Law, Before and After Maastricht* (Boston: Deventer, 1992), is revealing in this regard.

5. In a communication entitled "Nouvelles perspectives pour l'action de la Communauté dans le domaine culturel," COM(92) 149 final, 29 April 1992.

6. See M. Galle, "The European Parliament and the Role of Culture in Europe," in Bekemans, ed., p. 113.

7. Loman et al., p. 197, n. 46.

8. As Christopher Ansell (Department of Political Science, University of California, Berkeley) pointed out to me, on the basis of his own research.

9. "Eco will Europa mit Liebe machen"; published also in *Nordamerikanische Wochenpost*, 3 March 1995.

10. "Socrates at the Margin," *Times Higher Education Supplement*, 29 July 1994. See also L. Bekemans and M.-C. El Fallah-Bernard, "Des sciences sociales aux sciences humaines—Vers un nouvel humanisme," *Etude concernant l'enseignement des sciences économiques, sociales et politiques dans les universités en Europe* (report to the European Parliament, Luxembourg, Direction Générale des Etudes, Dir. A, Bruges, 1994), pp. 56–58.

11. COM(95) 110 final, 29 March 1995; currently still under consideration by the Council and the European Parliament.

12. In a proposal dating from 22 May 1995 (File no. 9501164).

13. For the issue of education, academic traditions, and culture in general, see P. Tabatoni, "L'Europe de l'enseignement supérieur: Vers une communauté des universités," in Picht, ed., pp. 127–52.

14. J. Vandamme, "Le rôle des petits pays dans la Communauté Européenne," *L' Avenir d'une économie de petite espace dans l'Europe de demain* (Luxembourg, 1995), pp. 11–14.

THE EUROPEAN UNION BETWEEN FEDERALISM AND REGULATION

James A. Caporaso

On 6–7 November 1995 a number of participants attended a conference at the University of California, Berkeley, to discuss the broad theme, "European Integration and American Federalism: A Comparative Perspective." I welcomed the opportunity to participate in this conference, to exchange views with other participants, and to both enlarge and sharpen the terms of debate about the present and future political architecture of the European Union (EU).

For too long, debates over the basic political structure of the EU have been monopolized by intergovernmental and neofunctionalist models. Theoretical attempts to explain what takes place in the EU or among its member-states have assumed caricatured shapes and have overly simplified very complex processes. Intergovernmental models sometimes approach the drama of an American Western, with high-stakes confrontations among members mimicking high-noon shootouts. By contrast, neofunctionalist models mindlessly portray how elbow-rubbing in Brussels creates transnational and supranational elites out of private and public actors and how the socializing process is ultimately subversive of loyalties to nation-states.

Happily, the proceedings of the conference escaped polarized debate and concentrated instead on the utility and limitations of the federal model for understanding European integration. Most—though not all—of the attention focused on American federalism, though the German model, with a different emphasis on constituent representation in the Bundesrat, surfaced a number of times.

My goal in this short paper is to discuss the idea of a federal system or "federalizing process" as it relates to the process of integration in the EU, to point out some strengths and limitations, and to offer another approach which, while not incompatible with federalism, nevertheless has a distinct emphasis.

FEDERALISM AND THE "FEDERALIZING" PROCESS

The term "federal" identifies a particular type of system of governance, one in which powers and competencies are allocated along a territorial dimension between central (sometimes confusingly called "federal") and outlying (states, provinces, cantons) units. While the exact nature of the assigned powers is open, federalism generally implies three things: formal assignment of powers so that the central and constituent units are supreme in some areas (and share competencies in others); inability to alter this constitutional arrangement without the consent of both central and constituent units; and a written constitution, almost a necessity since the other two points need to be clear, objective, and formal.

The above provides a rather strict (and hence narrow) definition of federalism. Federalism can be conceived more broadly as a system of governance balancing territorial interests, often along with other (e.g., functional) interests (Sbragia 1993). Daniel Elazar has detached federalism from the federal process:

> The federal principle does not necessarily mean establishing a federal system in the conventional sense of a modern federal state. The essence of federalism is not to be found in a particular set of institutions but in the institutionalization of particular relationships among the participants in political life. Consequently, federalism is a phenomenon that provides many options for the organization of political authority and power (Elazar 1987: 11–12).

This broader conceptualization of federalism allows us to employ an analogy organized on the principle of cross-level relationships without subscribing to the specific institutional requirements of federal systems. The analogy might be helpful in exploring the territorial dynamics of unitary systems (subsidiarity, for example, often comes up in the context of the United Kingdom, a unitary state) or the relationships among multiple levels of governance in inchoate systems such as the EU, where the predominant institutional form is still in doubt. Such an orientation seems central to the work of Pierson and Leibfried (1995) and Marks (1993).

Federalism refers to a system of governance designed to accommodate differences where those differences are grouped more or less homogeneously by territory. The spatial distribution of differences is critical. Where cleavages are functional (based on roles and performance of tasks), sectoral, or based on class antagonisms, the federal principle will not work.

EVALUATION AND CRITIQUE

The federal idea seems highly relevant for the EU, where constituent units are territorially organized nation-states. As Sbragia has insightfully pointed out, the EU is a political construction that strives to balance territorial and nonterritorial claims. Most of the institutions of the community have a territorial aspect, most pronounced in the cases of the Council of Ministers and the European Council, least evident in the cases of the Economic and Social Committee and the European Commission. Even the judges of the European Court of Justice (ECJ) are appointed by member governments. Members of Parliament, while they organize and "sit" according to political party affiliation, are "elected within national boundaries according to national electoral laws and paid according to national pay scales, and the seventeen commissioners who make up the European Commission (the Community's executive) are each appointed by their national government" (Sbragia 1993: 28).

The limits of the federal idea are also apparent. While the ECJ may be creating a federal constitution out of an intergovernmental treaty, its reach (i.e., its jurisdiction) is more narrow than often admitted. In addition, many of the competencies that exist within EU institutions rest upon delegated powers—i.e., powers that the member-states have ceded to international institutions under carefully circumscribed conditions. These assignments of "authority" are retractable, unlike those that belong to units in federal systems. Delegated authority is "power on a leash." This is different from the federal conception in which central and local units are superior within identified spheres and where these authority relations cannot be changed except by joint agreement of central and local units.

There is another reason why the federal idea provides only a partial understanding, and this has to do with the fact that in a substantial number of areas, policy is increasingly detached from territory. This is true for the most inclusive public goods (environment, security, technical standards), as well as for a growing number of regulatory issues "governed" by special purpose agencies. It is not that these issues do not have a territorial component (they all do), but that the link between territory and policy is not so manageable as arenas such as agriculture and regional policy. Clean air and water are issues that make their mark across national divides; appropriate labels for food and drugs, health and safety standards, and regulations for railroads are not easily confined to national territorial boundaries. The point is not that policies are always "community-wide," based on a public indivisibility that glides over national differences. Rather, there is an increasing number of cases where policy goals cannot be achieved except by overall collective action, often because of strategic gains to be reaped by member-states who do not cooperate (while others do, a prisoner's dilemma).

AN ALTERNATIVE VIEW

Students of federalism have pressed the domestic analogy, or rather one version of it. Realists, on the other hand, have insisted on the essentially intergovernmental character of the EU, arguing that policy outcomes (especially the big ones) are due to the power and interests of the important member-states.

It was natural that the first wave of scholarship on European integration searched for an appropriate model within the inventory of current (and past) forms of government. The EU was seen as falling short of a mature state, but this reflected its early stage of development. Its basic genetic blueprint was federal. It just needed time to elaborate its imminent structure. However, this approach raises a troubling anomaly. The EU's institutions and policies are systematically different from those of national governments, not only in the areas mentioned, but also in the basic profile of activities and competencies. The EU's portfolio of functions and responsibilities differs radically and is not explicable by its less advanced position on the continuum of development. According to this view, the EU is not a primitive national political system waiting to blossom. The EU is weak in terms of the traditional tax and spend functions of government. The extractive capacity of EU institutions is nearly zero, reflecting a stalemate going back to Hallstein's failed "own resources" initiative in 1965, one of the factors precipitating the empty chair crisis. The EU spends about 1.3 percent of combined gross domestic product (gdp) of its member-states and accounts for about 4 percent of government spending (Majone 1994c: 35). The Commission, Europe's chief administrative and regulatory apparatus, is modestly staffed by approximately 20,000 people, of whom about one-third are translators. Despite occasional pre-dawn raids by the Commission, the EU is hardly a well-heeled Leviathan.

Yet the EU is generally recognized as an important institution. Why? One answer to the paradox of "marginal spending cum recognized importance" lies in conceiving the EU as a regulatory state. The regulatory state is (in this case) essentially an international and arguably supranational state specializing in the control and management of international externalities. Because this state does not engage substantially in the redistributive, stabilization, and symbolic functions of government, and because it relies on the administrative structures of states already in place to carry out its own policies rather than on independent ones created at the supranational level, the international state can "get by" with a very small revenue base.

Acceptance of the regulatory state as a useful description of the EU has broad implications. The first implication is that we should not expect the EU to look like a traditional nation-state at all, nor its future development to follow the beaten path from intergovernmental relations to confederation to federation. Instead we should expect a political division of labor between member-states, focusing on social and redistributional policy, and the EU , focusing on regulatory policy. From this angle, it would be theoretically misplaced to judge development of the EU in terms of the growth of its taxing and spending powers. Its weakness in terms of extraction and broad spending powers is not due to an "early state of development," nor are these functions likely to be supplied by the dynamics of functional linkages (spillover). The regulatory state is not the Westphalian state, the extractive state, or the social democratic state. Its future contours are not likely to resemble these state forms more than at present.

A second implication relates to the connection between regulatory structures and democracy, an issue all the more salient because of the debate over the democratic deficit. Given the weakness of European parties, the strength of specialized interest groups, the under-representation of large unconcentrated groups, the secrecy of the Council, and the unpopular nature of the Commission and the Court, we should ask what effect the increase of international regulatory structures will have.

In the United States regulatory structures were created in part to avoid the swings of public opinion and to insulate agencies from Madisonian factions. Agencies were even placed outside the hierarchy of presidential control (Majone 1994b: 17). The proliferation of agencies in the United States has been attacked on the grounds that agencies constitute a nonrepresentative fourth branch of government, undermining the separation of powers and placing government further beyond the reach of private citizens. While Majone's work attempts to reconcile independence and accountability—as they can be in principle—I believe he understates the antidemocratic possibilities of independent regulatory agencies. Even Majone, whose treatment of regulation policy is sympathetic, sees dangers resulting from a lack of transparency in regulatory structures (1994a: 41).

While provision of transparency would be a step in the right direction, it would have only a limited effect. A deeper problem is that the EU is only a partial—one might even say "truncated"—political system. It lacks a broad, representative parliament with real capacity for law-making. It lacks a European dimension to its party system, with the result that group interests are not assembled into broad and coherent programs. The consequence is a weakening of public discussion and a failure of the EU to take on popular meaning in terms of our most significant ideological dimensions (left-right, populist-elitist, activist-limited role for state). If the EU is a limited, market-perfection project, this would seem borne out by limited mass public engagement in European issues.

The federal model is particularly appropriate for understanding relations among levels of government organized territorially. If the evolving EU can be seen as a system of multilevel governance (Marks

1993) or the central component of "an emergent multitiered system of governance" (Pierson and Leibfried 1995: 3), traditional models of federal relations should be analytically useful. Territorial politics continue to be important in the EU. In addition, more energy should be spent identifying alternative forms of collective governance and authority whose structures appear state-like in almost every respect. One such form of international governance is illustrated by the numerous forms of regulatory decision-making in the EU.

The regulatory state lacks a neat pyramidal structure of power; there are no clear architectural lines of authority attached to it, nor any bold constitutional statement of the relations between citizen and state. The original democratic problem, expressed in the modern language of principal-agent theory, is how to establish a government to solve the problems of the people without becoming a creature serving its own interests. This problem is now complicated by another contractual issue—namely, how can the state (society's agent) delegate limited authority to international regulatory bodies that effectively serve the state's interests? The "people," sovereign in democratic theory, are now twice removed from the agents supposedly acting on their behalf.

Federalism, conceived broadly as a framework for understanding territorial politics, continues to be important for understanding complex relations among supranational, national, and subnational levels of government. But emerging forms of governance are too complex to be captured exclusively by federal models, no matter how broadly defined. The sharpest challenge posed by the EU is to understand the most advanced (modern) forms of political authority, only partially captured by our metaphors and frameworks shaped by the past.

REFERENCES

Elazar, Daniel J. 1987. *Exploring Federalism.* Tuscaloosa: University of Alabama Press, 1987.

Majone, Giandomenico. 1994a. "The European Community: An 'Independent Fourth Branch of Government'?" In *Verfassungen fur ein ziviles Europa,* ed. Gert Bruggemeier. Baden-Baden, Germany: Nomos Verlagsgesellschaft, pp. 23–43.

———. 1994b. "Independence vs. Accountability? Non-Majoritarian Institutions and Democratic Government in Europe." EUI Working Papers in Political and Social Sciences, European University Institute, pp. 1–29.

———. 1994c. "Paradoxes of Privatization and Deregulation." *Journal of European Public Policy* 1, 1: 53–69.

Marks, Gary. 1993. "Structural Policy and Multilevel Governance in the EC." In *The State of the European Community*, vol. 2, ed. Alan W. Cafrung and Glenda G. Rosenthal, pp. 391–410. Boulder, Colo.: Lynne Rienner.

Pierson, Paul, and Stephan Leibfried. 1995. "Multitiered Institutions and the Making of Social Policy." In *European Social Policy: Between Fragmentation and Integration*, ed. Stephan Leibfried and Paul Pierson, pp. 1–40. Washington, D.C.: Brookings Institution.

Sbragia, Alberta M. 1993. "The European Community: A Balancing Act." *Publius* 23, 3: 23–38.

INTERLOCKING POLITICS AND THE EUROPEAN UNION

Thomas Risse-Kappen

The European Union's (EU) Single Market program as well as the Maastricht treaties on the EU and Economic and Monetary Union (EMU) have led to a revival of the scholarly debate on the nature of European integration. Many scholars are increasingly dissatisfied with traditional approaches conceptualizing the EU in neofunctionalist or intergovernmentalist terms. Notions such as "pooling of sovereignty" (Keohane and Hoffmann 1991), "multi-level governance" (Marks 1993), *"Fusionsthese"* (Wessels 1992), or "policy networks" (Héritier 1993a; Héritier, ed. 1993; Peterson 1995; Scharpf 1993) indicate an emerging consensus that the boundaries between the "domestic" and the "international" spheres as well as between the "state" and "society" have to be crossed when talking about the EU.

This paper attempts to clarify some issues involved in this mode of new thinking about the EU. I present a framework for analyzing the EU which combines insights from recent work on transnational politics among international relations scholars, on policy networks as well as *Politikverflechtung* (interlocking politics) in the field of comparative policy analysis, and from historical institutionalism. I generate propositions on the institutional and structural conditions under which network analysis appears to be better suited than intergovernmentalism to capture the distinctive features of the EU policy-making process.

NEW THINKING ABOUT THE EU IN INTERNATIONAL RELATIONS THEORY AND COMPARATIVE POLICY ANALYSIS

Scholars in international relations and in comparative politics have become increasingly aware that the traditional notions of intergovernmental bargaining or supranationalism fail to capture the essence of EU decision-making. As a result, international relations and comparative politics scholars have begun to reconceptualize the EU. From an international relations perspective, recent work on *transnational relations* might be helpful. Transnational relations are defined as transboundary relations that include at least one nongovernmental actor (Kaiser 1969; Keohane and Nye, eds. 1971; Keohane and Nye 1977). Equally important in the context of the EU are *transgovernmental* relations—i.e., cross-boundary relations among subunits of national governments in the absence of centralized decisions by state executives (Keohane and Nye 1974). While the notion of transnational relations defies the idea of the state as the *only* significant actor in international relations, the concept of transgovernmental relations challenges the view that national governments can be treated as *unitary* actors.

The subject of transnational relations has recently been revived in international relations (Risse-Kappen, ed. 1995; for a recent application to the EU, see George 1994). This work moves beyond earlier attempts at theorizing about transnational relations in several ways:

1. While the concept of the state as the only important and unitary actor in world politics is given up, it is not eliminated altogether. Rather than replacing the state-dominated concept of international relations by a "society-centered" view of the world, research focuses on the interaction between states and transnational relations. If this concept were applied to the EU, one would stop arguing in an "either-or" fashion as if interstate bargaining were increasingly replaced by transnational and transgovernmental coalition-building. It is more interesting to ask how interstate relations (Council of Ministers and European Council), supranational bodies (European Commission, European Parliament [EP], European Court of Justice [ECJ]), and transnational/transgovernmental relations (the "comi-

tology" as well as interest group lobbying) interact to form the peculiar institutional structure of the EU (see Jachtenfuchs and Kohler-Koch 1996).

2. The new scholarship on transnational relations differentiates between the state as structure and governments as actors. Domestic structures—i.e., political institutions, structures of society, and state-society relations (Katzenstein, ed. 1978; Evangelista—forthcoming)—mediate and filter the influence of transnational relations on state policies by determining both access points for transnational actors and the size of "winning coalitions" necessary for policy impact. As to the EU, one would assume that the increasingly dense network of transnational coalitions and organizations—from transnational interest groups (Eising and Kohler-Koch 1994) to European party organizations—not only affects EU policies directly, but also the processes of national preference formation as mediated by the domestic structures of the member-states. Domestic structures also affect the very nature of transnational and/or transgovernmental actors (Krasner 1995). In the EU, for example, the German Bundesbank can act as a transnational actor precisely because the German political structure grants it independence from the national government (Cameron 1995).

3. The revival of research on transnational relations integrates studies on international institutions. The original regime literature was aware that highly institutionalized interstate relations provide an environment that allows transnational and transgovernmental relations to flourish (Keohane and Nye 1977; Keohane 1984). Recent research confirms the hypothesis (Cameron 1995; Katzenstein and Tsujinaka 1995; Risse-Kappen 1995). Since the EU represents the most densely institutionalized network of international regimes and organizations in the world, these findings challenge the intergovernmentalist hypothesis about EU policy-making.

In sum, recent progress in theorizing about transnational relations provides a starting point to conceptualize the EU from an international relations perspective. The new literature also allows for a fruitful dialogue with comparative politics where recent work closely resembles the studies on transnational relations and international institutions reviewed above:

1. Analysts increasingly view the EU as *a multilevel structure of governance* emphasizing horizontal and vertical linkages among substate and state actors. As Gary Marks, Liesbet Hooghe, and Kermit Blank put it,

> First, decision making competences are shared by actors at different levels rather than monopolized by state executives. . . . In the second place, political arenas are interconnected rather than nested. . . . [Subnational actors] act directly both in national and supranational arenas, creating transnational associations in the process. States do not monopolize links between domestic and European actors, but are one among a variety of actors contesting decisions that are made at a variety of levels (1994: 8; see also Marks 1993; Jachtenfuchs and Kohler-Koch, eds. 1996).

This closely resembles the notions of transnational and transgovernmental relations.

2. *Interorganizational network analysis* has become increasingly popular among comparative policy analysts to characterize the EU policy-making process. Policy networks are defined as nonhierarchical, decentralized, and mostly informal interaction patterns among actors—both individuals and corporate actors (organizations)—to solve collective action problems (Héritier 1993a: 432–33; Marsh and Rhodes, eds. 1992; Marin and Mayntz, eds. 1991; Mayntz 1993; Scharpf 1993). Policy networks describe structures of governance involving private and state actors linked together through varying degrees of resource dependencies that determine which actors dominate the network and how decisions are made.

These efforts at reconceptualizing policy-making in the EU beyond traditional notions of the state and of supranationalism can well be integrated in the concept of Politikverflechtung, which has become increasingly popular among German comparativists to characterize EU policy-making. Interlocking politics is defined as "the establishment of intermediating structures linking the politics—namely, the decision processes—and policies—the substantive responsibilities—of initially autonomous organizations" (Lehmbruch 1989; see also Scharpf 1994a).

The concept was originally used to analyze peculiar features of German federalism, particularly horizontal and vertical linkages among state and nonstate actors on the regional and national levels. Interlocking politics increasingly characterizes policy-making in various issue-areas of complex political systems in highly industrialized countries. National governments and bureaucracies regularly participate in these policy networks, but they are by no means the only significant actors. The similarities of these attempts to conceptualize modern policy-making with the notion of multilevel governance and with recent work on transnational relations are striking. If governance structures inside modern nation-states are increasingly characterized by informal patterns of interest mediation involving societal, political, and state actors, why should policy-making in the EU as a far less hierarchical system of governance than the nation-state be different?

There have been some attempts to apply network analysis to the EU. John Peterson (1995), for example, differentiates among various levels of decision-making in the EU. He argues that "history-making" decisions such as the Maastricht treaties can be well explained by neofunctionalism or intergovernmentalism, while network analysis would be applicable to "policy-shaping" affairs in the various sectors of EU policy-making. So far, network analysis has indeed been most successfully used to study sectoral policies in the EU. One of the most comprehensive studies pertains to environmental regulation (Héritier 1993a, 1993b; Héritier et al. 1995). While the level of institutionalization in this policy area is comparatively weak, the networks appear to be rather heterogenous and fluctuating as well as involving several levels of local, regional, national, transnational, and supranational actors. Strengthened by institutional rules such as the right to take initiatives, the European Commission turns out to be a central actor in the policy network and the main target of lobbying activities by transnational actors such as environmental organizations and business groups. Intergovernmental bargaining cannot be ignored in European environmental regulation, partly due to the organizational weakness of transnational interest groups (see also Kohler-Koch 1992). Héritier's findings essentially confirm the argument (Risse-Kappen, ed. 1995) that the emergence of strong transnational actors is correlated with the degree of institutionalization in a given issue-area.

Héritier's findings pertaining to the centrality of the European Commission in the EU policy networks have been confirmed for research and technology policies—another area in which the Commission has expanded its competences considerably (Grande 1992; Kohler-Koch 1994; Peschke 1994; Sandholtz 1992). In contrast to the findings pertaining to environmental regulation, however, the intergovernmental level of EU policy-making appeared to be less involved in European R&T policies. When the member-states tried to restrict the Commission's role in R&T, in particular its focus on industrial policy, the Commission moved its activities into areas where it enjoyed greater competences.

In sum, empirical studies underline Peterson's argument that network analysis can be applied with regard to sectoral policies in the EU. It is less clear, however, why multilevel governance, interlocking politics, and network analysis should be less suitable to the study of "history-making" decisions. It is plausible that such decisions involve interstate bargaining toward the final stages of the decision-making process and that these bargains can be less easily overturned than those emerging from policy networks. But it is not convincing to assume that decisions involving treaty-making and changes in the EU's institutional structure are confined to interstate bargaining through all stages of the decision-making process.

With regard to the Single European Act, for example, there is a lively debate on the role of supranational and transnational actors, on the one hand (Sandholtz and Zysman 1989; Cowles 1993), and interstate bargaining, on the other (Moravcsik 1991). Concerning the process leading to EMU, David Cameron (1995) has shown in detail that it cannot be explained without taking transnational and transgovernmental coalition-building into account. It is too simplistic to describe the EMU decision as a Franco-German deal resulting from a compromise between French (common currency) and German (convergence criteria) exogenously defined preferences. Germany did not behave as a unitary actor in the negotiations. Then Foreign Minister Genscher sided with Paris, favoring quick monetary union, while the Finance Ministry and the Bundesbank were initially opposed and then pushed hard for the convergence of economic policies prior to a common currency. Moreover, important bargaining processes leading to EMU took place in transnational settings that prepared the intergovernmental meetings of the European Council. This is not to suggest that intergovernmental bargaining was irrelevant in the process leading to EMU. Cameron proposes that transnational networking and intergovernmental negotiations were confined to different *stages* of the decision-making process.

In sum, there is a growing convergence among international relations and comparative politics scholars conceptualizing the EU as a multilevel structure of governance whereby private, governmental, transnational, and supranational actors deal with each other in highly complex networks of varying density as well as horizontal and vertical depth. But one should not throw out the baby with the bathwater. There might indeed be conditions under which an intergovernmentalist model of decision-making is more appropriate to understanding EU politics than overly complex network models. To move our theoretical understanding of the EU further, we need a set of hypotheses on the conditions under which multilevel governance rather than intergovernmentalism characterizes the EU policy-making process. In the following, I draw on insights from historical institutionalism (Steinmo et al., eds. 1992; for the EU, see Bulmer 1994) and from research on domestic structures in comparative foreign policy to develop such propositions.

MULTILEVEL GOVERNANCE IN THE EU: INSTITUTIONAL STRUCTURES AND ACTORS

My point of departure is Andrew Moravcsik's "liberal intergovernmentalist" framework (Moravcsik 1992, 1993, 1994), which represents a model of parsimony and clarity. His framework combines preference formation on the domestic level with intergovernmental bargaining on the international level to explain policy-making in the EU. In the following, my aim is to identify the conditions under which policy-making in the EU can be conceptualized in "liberal intergovernmentalist" terms and when this model is no longer sufficient and we need to add complexity in terms of multilevel governance and interlocking politics.

STRUCTURES OF GOVERNANCE IN THE EU I: THE IMPACT OF DOMESTIC STRUCTURES

Policy-making in the EU does not take place in an institutional void. The domestic structures of the member-states and the institutional structure of the EU exert independent effects on the ability of actors to shape the European policy agenda, to create "winning coalitions," to influence decisions, and to implement them. As to *domestic structures*, we need to differentiate among the structure of the political institutions, societal interest formation and aggregation, state-society relations, and the norms and values embedded in the political culture (Katzenstein, ed. 1978; Evangelista—forthcoming; Risse-Kappen, ed. 1995). Domestic structures not only vary among the member-states, but also with regard to the issue-areas involved. One would expect, for example, that national governments enjoy a comparatively higher degree of autonomy from society in national security affairs than, say, in the area of macroeconomic policies (but see Katzenstein and Tsujinaka 1995, concerning Japan). But it is open to debate whether the overall structure of the polity is more likely to determine politics in a given issue-area or whether specifics of the policy-arena are more significant. As to European policy-making, the domestic structures of the member-states are likely to affect

- the size of minimum winning support coalitions which national governments need to pursue effective policies in the EU—in other words, the degree of state autonomy from societal constraints;
- the extent to which national governments are able to act with one voice—as unitary actors—on the EU level;
- the degree to which transnational policy networks are likely to emerge involving domestic societal and political actors, on the one hand, and supranational EU actors, on the other, which might circumvent national governments as the major conveyor belts between domestic demands and the EU level;
- the extent to which these policy networks—rather than national governments—implement EU policies on the national level;
- the level of internalization of EU principles and norms in the domestic polity.

The following propositions can then be generated as to the effects of member-state domestic structures on EU policy-making:

1. *The more fragmented and decentralized the political institutions, the stronger the organization of societal interest representation, and the greater the consensus requirements in state-society relations, the less capa-*

ble are national governments to pursue independent and autonomous policies on the EU level.

It follows that national governments such as the German or the Dutch, operating in a domestic environment with a high degree of *interlocking politics,* should be less capable of pursuing autonomous strategies in the EU than, for example, the British or French. The latter act in a comparatively centralized institutional structure (France), a weakly organized structure of interest representation (Britain), and a comparatively polarized political culture (France and Britain). The second proposition is directly related to the first:

2. *The more fragmented and decentralized the political institutions and the stronger the organization of interest representation in society, the less likely are national governments to behave as unitary actors in the EU policy-making process and the more likely they are to externalize the lack of domestic consensus in a given policy-area onto the EU level.*

The German state serves again as a primary example to illustrate the point. As Cameron (1995) shows for the EMU decision, the Foreign Office, the Chancellerie, and the Bundesbank pursued quite different policies during the negotiations. The likelihood that transgovernmental coalitions will emerge on the EU level appears to be partly a function of the domestic political structure of the member-states.

But the nature of the domestic political institutions and the structure of societal interest formation and representation should affect not only the capacity of national governments to act autonomously and with one voice on the EU level. Recent work on transnational relations suggests that domestic structures also refract and mediate the policy impact of transnational actors by providing both access points to the national polities and determining the size of necessary "winning coalitions" (Krasner 1995; Risse-Kappen, ed. 1995). Applied to the EU, we should not expect the same level of transnational network density and depth in each member-state, irrespective of the domestic structure and the issue-area involved.

3. *The more fragmented the political institutions and the stronger the organization of societal interest representation, the more likely are transnational policy networks to emerge among EU institutions and political as well as societal actors in the member-states, and the more likely are these networks to affect EU policies.*

Research on transnational interest representation in Brussels has shown, for example, that "groups that are strongly entrenched in their respective state arena are more likely to be mobilized in the European arena than groups that are weakly represented in their respective state arena" (Marks et al. 1994: 35). Most interest groups represented in Brussels also play a significant role on the national level of interest representation. The density and the horizontal as well as vertical depth of the transnational networks should also vary depending on the issue-area involved.

STRUCTURES OF GOVERNANCE IN THE EU II: THE IMPACT OF EU INSTITUTIONS

Another structure of governance affecting EU policy-making consists of the institutional arrangements of the EU itself. The *acquis communautaire* contains an elaborate set of norms, rules, and decision-making procedures regulating the competences of the European Council, the Council of Ministers, the Commission, the EP, and the ECJ. If institutions matter, these decision-making regimes should have repercussions for the policy-making process and the actors involved—in a similar way as domestic political institutions. Institutionalism posits that transnational and transgovernmental networking is the more likely the more institutionalized and cooperatively regulated interstate relations are in a given issue-area. Applied to the EU, one would then assume that transnational and transgovernmental coalition-building rather than intergovernmental bargaining characterizes the EU policy-making process depending on the degree to which

- the respective issue-area or policy sector is regulated by EU policies;
- the respective policy-area is governed by majority rather than consensus rule in the Council.

This leads to the following proposition:

4. *The more a particular policy sector has been integrated and the more decisions in this area are governed by majority rule, the more likely it is that the policy-making process is characterized by transnational and transgovernmental coalitions among private, national, and supranational actors rather than intergovernmental bargaining.*

According to the hypothesis, one would expect transnational and transgovernmental decision-making in those issue-areas in which the Commission has the sole prerogative to take the iniative for EU action. There are about 500 expert groups that the Commission uses to prepare its initiatives and that link national bureaucracies, transnational interest groups, and the DGs in complex networks of varying density (Wessels 1992: 46; Bach 1992). The same holds true for the implementation procedures of EU decisions with the institutionalized "comitology" structure leading to more than 300 committees linking the Commission to the national bureaucracies of the member-states. This complex structure cannot be conceptualized as either intergovernmental or supranational, but appears to be truly transnational.

Moreover, the more integrated a given policy-area, the more one would expect from an institutionalist perspective that transnational structures of interest representation start to flourish. Since the European integration process has largely been about market integration, business interests are better represented by transnational organizations on the EU level than labor, and transnational business organizations such as UNICE have increasingly gained corporate actor qualities (Kohler-Koch 1992; Eising and Kohler-Koch 1994: 180–81). The same holds true for agricultural interests in the context of the Common Agricultural Policy (overview in Kohler-Koch 1992: 98–101). But even the rather weakly institutionalized EU social policy has already affected the institutional structure of the European Federation of Trade Unions and its relations to the national labor organizations (Armigeon 1994; Miller 1995; Sörries 1995).

This still leaves the "history-making" decisions as well as those issue-areas that are only loosely integrated. As to the latter, one would probably not expect dense transnational and transgovernmental policy networks to prevail in the Common Foreign and Security Policy (CFSP). The CFSP seems to remain a policy-area where intergovernmental bargaining dominates the decision-making process. With regard to "history-making" decisions, it would depend on whether these decisions move the integration process further along in already institutionalized policy-areas or whether they "Europeanize" new issues. The decision on the second pillar of the Maastricht treaties—political union instituting the CFSP—represents an example for the latter, while the move from EMS to EMU appears to characterize the former case.

The decisions leading to EMU took place within the densely institutionalized regime structure provided by the EMS. This process represented a complex sequence of transgovernmental negotiations, intergovernmental bargaining, and consent, as well as domestic ratification by the member-states (Cameron 1995).

The following table summarizes the argument how the member-state domestic structures, on the one hand, and the EU institutional structure, on the other, together determine the degree to which governance in the EU can be modeled as intergovernmental bargaining or transnational and transgovernmental networking. Of course the table is overly simplistic. Both dimensions of variables should be read as continuums. The table easily accommodates Peterson's (1995) distinctions among "history-making," "policy-setting," and "policy-shaping" EU decisions and can then be read as follows:

Table 1

Structures of Governance and Policy-Making in the EU

Domestic Structure	Degree of "Europeanization" of Issue Area	
	Stronger	Weaker
Fragmented political institutions Strong societal organizations	Transnational and transgovernmental policy networks (Interlocking politics)	Intermediate level of network density and depth
⋮	⋮	⋮
Centralized political institutions Weak social interests	Low network density and depth	Intergovernmental bargaining

- Concerning "policy-shaping" EU decisions and the implementation of EU regulations, one would expect a high degree of interlocking politics (northwestern cell of the table) since such processes involve both Europeanized issue-areas and all member-states, including those with fragmented polities.

- With regard to "history-making" and "policy-setting" decisions, we would expect variation, depending on

a) the domestic structure of those member-states involved in the major bargains;

b) the degree of previous Europeanization—institutional path dependence—of the policy area to be regulated.

For example, if Britain and France are the major players in a decision-making process in a previously weakly regulated policy area, we would expect intergovernmental bargaining to prevail (southeastern cell). If, however, Germany is heavily involved in a policy-shaping decision regarding an already Eu ropeanized issue-area, we would again expect interlocking politics.

CONCLUSIONS: SOME POLICY CONSIDERATIONS

This article has tried to identify the conditions under which EU policy-making can be better explained as a system of multilevel governance consisting of various degrees of transnational and transgovernmental Politikverflechtung rather than intergovernmental bargaining. If one moves from an analytical to a normative perspective, the dual problems of *efficiency* and *democracy* require further attention. As Fritz Scharpf already argued in 1985, processes of interlocking politics of varying density and depth make policy-making so complex involving so many actors that efficiency suffers. While the Europeanization of domestic policies moves entire issue-areas out of the competence of national governments and national decision-making, this does not necessarily increase the ability of the EU to take decisive action in a multilevel system of governance (Scharpf 1994a: 131-32).

Scharpf's "joint decision trap" argument is not necessarily convincing. It is not a priori clear that nonhierarchical structures of decision-making based on intra- and interorganizational networks are by and large less efficient than hierarchical structures such as intergovernmentalism in the case of the EU. The more EU decisions are based on intergovernmental bargaining and "two-level games" and the less informal networking takes place in the initiation and preparatory stages, the more likely it is that the resulting policies represent nothing more than the lowest common denominator and that decision blockades can be avoided only through extensive as well as expensive package deals (see Moravcsik 1993, but also Scharpf 1994b). Compare the slow-moving CFSP based on intergovernmental bargaining with the comparatively smooth operation of EU policies in highly integrated sectors. Moreover, joint decision traps can be avoided by exploiting the advantage of informal networks over formalized bargaining in that the former rather than the latter allow for systematically incorporating deliberative processes.

The *democracy* problem is more serious since it challenges the very basis of the Europeanization process. From the beginning, the vision of Europe was related to notions of liberal democracy and (social) market economy. But, as Karl Kaiser pointed out more than twenty years ago (1971), transnational politics tend to weaken democratic accountability by increasing the power of technocratic expert coalitions. While the Europeanization of domestic policies does not necessarily strengthen the state as a unitary actor, multilevel governance in transnational and transgovernmental networks appears to weaken the capability of democratically elected bodies on the local, regional, and national levels to control the process. Executives on the various levels of governance, expert communities, and technocrats seem to be strengthened. To cite just one example (Börzel 1995): As a result of the ratification of the Maastricht treaties, the German *Länder* have considerably increased their competence with regard to European politics, including securing a place at the table of the Council of Ministers. First experiences with the new decision-making structure show an increased level of horizontal Politikverflechtung between the German states and the federal government concerning European affairs. But the new structure strengthens national and state executives at the expense of both national parliaments and state legislatures.

What can be done? Some argue (for example, Scharpf 1994b: 131–55) that European integration should respect the autonomy of the nation-states, where democratic governance based on collective identities of the citizens is better secured than on the EU level. In other words, one should increase the intergovernmental character of the EU and decrease the significance of transnational and transgovernmental networks which appear to be outside democratic control. As Michael Zürn (1995) has convincingly argued, the flip side of this proposal is that it tends to strengthen the role and the autonomy of the national executives vis-à-vis their societies, as a result of which democratic accountability will be further weakened. The more national governments are the main transmission belts between domestic societies and international institutions and the more transnational links among societies and those between them and supranational institutions are reduced, the easier it is for national executives to control and manipulate the power resources of initiative, institutions, information, and ideas (Moravcsik 1994).

How can a complex structure of policy networks of varying density and depth be democratized (see also Schmitter 1996)?

1. Strengthening the competence of parliamentary bodies with regard to European affairs—from the EP and the national legislatures down to the city councils—appears to be a most urgent requirement to increase democratic rule in the EU. Note that a multilevel system of governance implies enlarging the role of parliaments on all levels of governance, not just the EP. Some efforts have already been made in conjunction with the ratification of the Maastricht treaties (Kupfer 1995).

2. Citizen participation in the networks preparing and implementing EU policies in the various policy sectors should be systematically strengthened. One way to do this would be to include representatives of public interest groups, social movement organizations, and others in these networks and to strengthen their links with supranational institutions such as the Commission. Moreover, why not use the model of the Social Dialogue between business and trade unions on the EU level in other sectors such as the environment?

3. Publicity is of utmost importance to democratize a multilevel system of governance. As long as European affairs have not been subject to public debate in the member-states, technocratic solutions by transnational and transgovernmental expert coalitions might prevail in a public climate of "permissive consensus." The Maastricht controversies seem to have changed this, at least to some extent, and to have politicized European affairs. It remains to be seen what the long-term consequences of this politicization will be.

Whatever solutions might be possible to alleviate the "democratic deficit," the consequences of ignoring it are disastrous. The EU currently faces a legitimacy crisis in most member-states. If nothing is done about it, the result is probably not a recourse to national solutions. There are no national solutions available for the problems facing Europe these days. Nongovernability will be the likely consequence, leading to a situation in which neither the member-states nor the EU can satisfy the demands of their citizens.

This is an abbreviated version of my article "Exploring the Nature of the Beast: International Relations Theory and Comparative Policy Analysis Meet the European Union," *Journal of Common Market Studies* 34, 1 (March 1996): 53–80.

REFERENCES

Armigeon, K. 1994. "Die Regulierung der kollektiven Arbeitsbeziehungen in der Europäischen Union." In Streeck, ed., pp. 207–22.

Bach, M. 1992. "Eine leise Revolution durch Verwaltungsverfahren: Bürokratische Integrationsprozesse in der Europäischen Gemeinschaft." *Zeitschrift für Soziologie* 21, 1: 16–30.

Börzel, T. 1995. "Does the European Integration Really Strengthen the State? The Case of the Federal Republic of Germany." Paper presented at Second Pan-European Conference in International Relations, Paris, 13–16 September.

Bulmer, S. 1994. "The Governance of the European Union: A New Institutionalist Approach." *Journal of Public Policy* 13, 4: 351–80.

Cameron, D. 1995. "Transnational Relations and the European Economic and Monetary Union." In Risse-Kappen, ed., pp. 37–78.

Cowles, M. L. G. 1993. "Setting the Agenda for a New Europe: The Politics of Big Business in EC 1992." Paper presented at Third Biennial Conference of the European Community Studies Association, Washington, D.C., 27–29 May.

Eising, R., and Kohler-Koch, B. 1994. "Inflation und Zerfaserung: Trends der Interessenvermittlung in der Europäischen Gemeinschaft." In Streeck, ed., pp. 175–206.

Evangelista, M. Forthcoming. "Domestic Structures and International Relations." In *New Thinking in International Relations Theory*, ed. Michael Doyle and G. John Ikenberry.

George, S. 1994. "Supranational Actors and Domestic Politics: Integration Theory Reconsidered in the Light of the Single European Act and Maastricht." Sheffield: University of Sheffield. Sheffield Papers in International Studies, No. 22.

Grande, E. 1992. *Die Forschungs- und Technologiepolitik der Europäischen Gemeinschaft: Programme und Aktivitäten im Bereich der Informations- und Kommunikationstechnik.* Cologne: Max-Planck-Institut für Gesellschafts Forschung.

Héritier, A. 1993a. "Policy-Netzwerkanalyse als Untersuchungsinstrument im europäischen Kontext: Folgerungen aus einer empirischen Studie regulativer Politik." In Héritier, ed., pp. 432–47.

———. 1993b. "Die Europäische Gemeinschaft als Faktor nationaler Politik: Hierarchisierung oder Dezentrie rung?" In *Politik und Technologieentwicklung in Europa*, ed. Werner Süß and Gerhard Becher. Berlin: Duncker and Humblot, pp. 105–29.

Héritier, A., et al. 1995. *Die Veränderung von Staatlichkeit in Europa.* Opladen: Westdeutscher Verlag.

Héritier, A., ed. 1993. *Policy-Analyse.* Opladen: Westdeutscher Verlag. Politische Vierteljahresschrift, Sonderheft 24.

Jachtenfuchs, M., and Kohler-Koch, B. 1996. "Einleitung: Regieren im dynamischen Mehrebenensystem." In Jachtenfuchs and Kohler-Koch, eds., pp. 15–44.

Jachtenfuchs, M., and Kohler-Koch, B., eds. 1996. *Europäische Integration.* Opladen: Leske and Budrich.

Kaiser, K. 1969. "Transnationale Politik." In *Die anachronistische Souveränität*, ed. Ernst-Otto Czempiel. Opladen: Westdeutscher Verlag, pp. 80–109.

———. 1971. "Transnational Relations as a Threat to the Democratic Process." In Keohane and Nye, eds., pp. 356–70.

Katzenstein, P. J., and Tsujinaka, Y. 1995. "'Bullying,' 'Buying,' and 'Binding': Transnational Relations, Domestic Structures, and the U.S.-Japanese Relationship." In Risse-Kappen, ed., pp. 79–111.

Katzenstein, P. J., ed. 1978. *Between Power and Plenty.* Madison, Wisc.: University of Wisconsin Press.

Keohane, R. O. 1984. *After Hegemony.* Princeton, N.J.: Princeton University Press.

Keohane, R. O., and Hoffmann, S. 1991. "Institutional Change in Europe in the 1980s." In *The New European Community*, ed. R. O. Keohane and S. Hoffmann. Boulder, Colo.: Westview, pp. 1–39.

Keohane, R., and Nye, J. S., Jr. 1974. "Transgovernmental Relations and International Organizations." *World Politics* 27: 39–62.

———. 1977. *Power and Interdependence.* Boston: Little, Brown.

Keohane, R. O., and Nye, J. S., Jr., eds. 1971. *Transnational Relations and World Politics.* Cambridge, Mass.: Harvard University Press.

Kohler-Koch, B. 1992. "Interessen und Integration. Die Rolle organisierter Interessen im westeuropäischen Integrations prozeß." In Kreile, ed., pp. 81–119.

———. 1994. "Das Vernetzungskonzept in der Forschungs- und Technologiepolitik der Europäischen Ge meinschaft." Manuscript, Mannheim, August.

Krasner, S. D. 1995. "Power Politics, Institutions and Transnational Relations." In Risse-Kappen, ed., pp. 257–79.

Kreile, M., ed. 1992. *Die Integration Europas*. Opladen: Westdeutscher Verlag. Politische Vierteljahresschrift, Sonderheft 23.

Kupfer, S. 1995. "Europäische Integration und parlamentarische Demokratie: Implikationen und Reaktionen am Beispiel des deutschen Bundestages." Diploma thesis, Fakultät für Verwaltungswissenschaft, Universität Konstanz.

Lehmbruch, G. 1989. "Institutional Linkages and Policy Networks in the Federal System of West Germany." *Publius: The Journal of Federalism* 19 (Fall): 221–35.

Marks, G. 1993. "Structural Policy and Multilevel Governance in the EC." In *The State of the European Community II: The Maastricht Debates and Beyond*, ed. Alan Cafruny and Glenda Rosenthal. Boulder, Colo.: Lynne Rienner.

Marks, G.; Hooghe, L.; and Blank, K. 1994. "European Integration and the State." Paper presented at American Political Science Association meeting, New York, 1–4 September.

Marin, B., and Mayntz, R., eds. 1991. *Policy Networks: Empirical Evidence and Theoretical Considerations*. Frankfurt/M.: Campus.

Marsh, D., and Rhodes, R. A. W., eds. 1992. *Policy Networks in British Government*. Oxford: Oxford University Press.

Mayntz, R. 1993. "Policy-Netzwerke und die Logik von Verhandlungssystemen." In Héritier, ed., pp. 39–56.

Miller, C. 1995. "Perspektiven europäischer Kollektivverhandlungen: Der 'Soziale Dialog' der Dachverbände der europäischen Sozialpartner und der sektorale Dialog im Chemie-und im Metallsektor." Diploma thesis, Fakultät für Verwaltungswissenschaft, Universität Konstanz.

Milward, A. S. 1992. *The European Rescue of the Nation-State*. Berkeley: University of California Press.

Moravcsik, A. 1991. "Negotiating the Single European Act." *International Organization* 45, 1: 19–56.

―――. 1992. "Liberalism and International Relations Theory." Cambridge, Mass.: Harvard University, Center for International Affairs. Working paper.

―――. 1993. "Preferences and Power in the European Community: A Liberal Intergovernmentalist Approach." *Journal of Common Market Studies* 31, 4: 473–524.

―――. 1994. "Why the European Community Strengthens the State: Domestic Politics and International Cooperation." Paper presented at Conference of Europeanists, Chicago, April.

Peschke, A. 1994. "Veränderungen in der Forschungs- und Technologiepolitik der Europäischen Union: Eine Analyse der Förderprogramme zur Ausbildung und Mobilität der Wissenschaftler." Diploma thesis, Fakultät für Verwaltungswissenschaft, Universität Konstanz.

Peterson, J. 1995. "Decision-Making in the European Union: Towards a Framework for Analysis." *Journal of European Public Policy* 2, 1: 69–93.

Risse-Kappen, T. 1995. *Cooperation among Democracies: The European Influence on U.S. Foreign Policy.* Princeton, N.J.: Princeton University Press.

———, ed. 1995. *Bringing Transnational Relations Back In: Non-State Actors, Domestic Structures, and International Institutions.* Cambridge: Cambridge University Press.

Sandholtz, W. 1992. *High-Tech Europe: The Politics of International Cooperation.* Berkeley: University of California Press.

Sandholtz, W., and Zysman, J. 1989. "1992: Recasting the European Bargain." *World Politics* 42: 95–128.

Scharpf, F. W. 1985. "Die Politikverflechtungsfalle: Europäische Integration und deutscher Föderalismus im Vergleich" *Politische Vierteljahresschrift* 26, 4: 323–56.

———. 1993. "Positive und negative Koordination in Verhandlungssystemen." In Héritier, ed., pp. 57–83.

———. 1994a. *Optionen des Föderalismus in Deutschland und Europa.* Frankfurt/M: Campus.

———. 1994b. "Mehrebenenpolitik im vollendeten Binnenmarkt." Discussion paper, Max-Planck-Institut für Gesellschaftsforschung, Cologne.

Schmitter, P. 1996. "Is It Possible to Democratize the Euro-Polity? If So, What Role Might Euro-Citizens Play in It?" Manuscript, Stanford University.

Sörries, B. 1995. "Die autonome Regelungskompetenz der europäischen Sozialpartner im Rahmen des Sozialen Dialogs." Diploma thesis, Fakultät für Verwaltungswissenschaft, Universität Konstanz.

Steinmo, S.; Thelen, K.; and Longstreth, F., eds. 1992. *Structuring Politics: Historical Institutionalism in Comparative Analysis.* Cambridge: Cambridge University Press.

Streeck, W., ed. 1994. *Staat und Verbände.* Opladen: Westdeutscher Verlag. Politische Vierteljahresschrift, Sonderheft 25.

Wessels, W. 1992. "Staat und (westeuropäische) Integration: Die Fusionsthese." In Kreile, ed., pp. 36–61.

Zürn, Michael. 1995. "Über den Staat und die Demokratie in der Europäischen Union." Manuscript, University of Bremen.

SOLVING MAASTRICHT'S FISCAL PROBLEM

Barry Eichengreen, Jürgen von Hagen, and Ian Harden

The debate over the fiscal provisions of the Maastricht Treaty is rapidly reaching a crescendo. Recent pronouncements by German officials have left no doubt that they will insist on strict application of the treaty's 3 and 60 percent reference values for government deficits and debts that the treaty sets down as preconditions for participation in EMU. The Bundestag and the German Constitutional Court have made clear that they will not accede to Germany's participation on other terms. And German officials have recently escalated their demands, insisting that meeting the debt and deficit limits in Stage II is not enough. Safeguards and penalties to ensure that countries also pursue sound fiscal policies in Stage III, when monetary union has commenced, must be strengthened as well.

This insistence on strict application of the reference values in Stage II is designed to bar from EMU countries reluctant to live with the budgetary implications of monetary union. Requiring them to balance their budgets in Stage III or else to incur harsh fines, or even expulsion from EMU, is intended to minimize the risk that countries will experience a Mexico-style debt crisis and ask for a bailout from the European Central Bank (ECB), pressuring the latter into inflationary policies.

Unfortunately, there is reason to doubt that the Maastricht criteria will achieve their aims. The treaty's deficit and debt limits are like the hurdles of a steeplechase. Set them too low and you learn nothing about the ability of the horses to jump. Set them too high and you again learn nothing since all the competitors balk when they are approached.

It is now evident that the framers of the Maastricht Treaty made this last mistake. Belgium and France, though committed to monetary union and prepared to live with its fiscal consequences, find themselves incapable of meeting the requirements. Even the Netherlands, which is all but in a monetary union with Germany already, will find it difficult to meet the debt limit by 1999.

The problem is that fiscal retrenchment of the sort required to bring debts and deficits down to 60 and 3 percent would plunge Europe into recession. Figures 1 and 2 show the severity of the recessions implied by fiscal retrenchment on the scale implied by the 3 percent deficit limits. (These simulations are reported in full in von Hagen and Lutz 1995 and Eichengreen and von Hagen 1995.) The simulations utilize John Taylor's (1993) G7 model. Taylor's model can be understood as a dynamic version of the Mundell-Fleming framework augmented by an aggregate supply curve. It consists of seven country models (including Germany, France, Italy, and the UK) linked together by capital and trade flows and features rational expectations in consumption, investment, the labor market, and the financial sector. While price and wage stickiness implies the short-run non-neutrality of nominal shocks, long-run neutrality is imposed in estimation.

With the addition of policy reaction functions, simulations can be performed assuming either flexible exchange rates or an EMS scenario in which intra-European exchange rates are pegged. In the baseline run, fiscal policy is characterized by a constant ratio of government spending to GNP. Monetary policy is governed by a constant growth rate of the money supply, producing an inflation rate of 4 percent in all countries. The baseline assumes output growth rates of 2.5 percent (France), 2.0 percent (Germany), 2.2 percent (Italy), and 1.5 percent (UK).

The simulations assume that government deficits are reduced to a maximum of 3 percent of GDP in the four EU economies. Deficit reduction is implemented by means of a cut in the government expenditure relative to GDP. The requisite cuts are 1 percent in France, 1 percent in Germany, 4 percent in Italy, and 2 percent in the UK. Thus the simulations allow us to compare countries undergoing modest adjustments (Germany and France) with others of which major adjustments are required. Spending cuts are phased in over five quarters, and the public learns about the policy four quarters in advance. We compare a flexible exchange rate regime with an EMS scenario in which exchange rates among European countries are fixed; this allows us to evaluate the exchange-rate criterion for entry

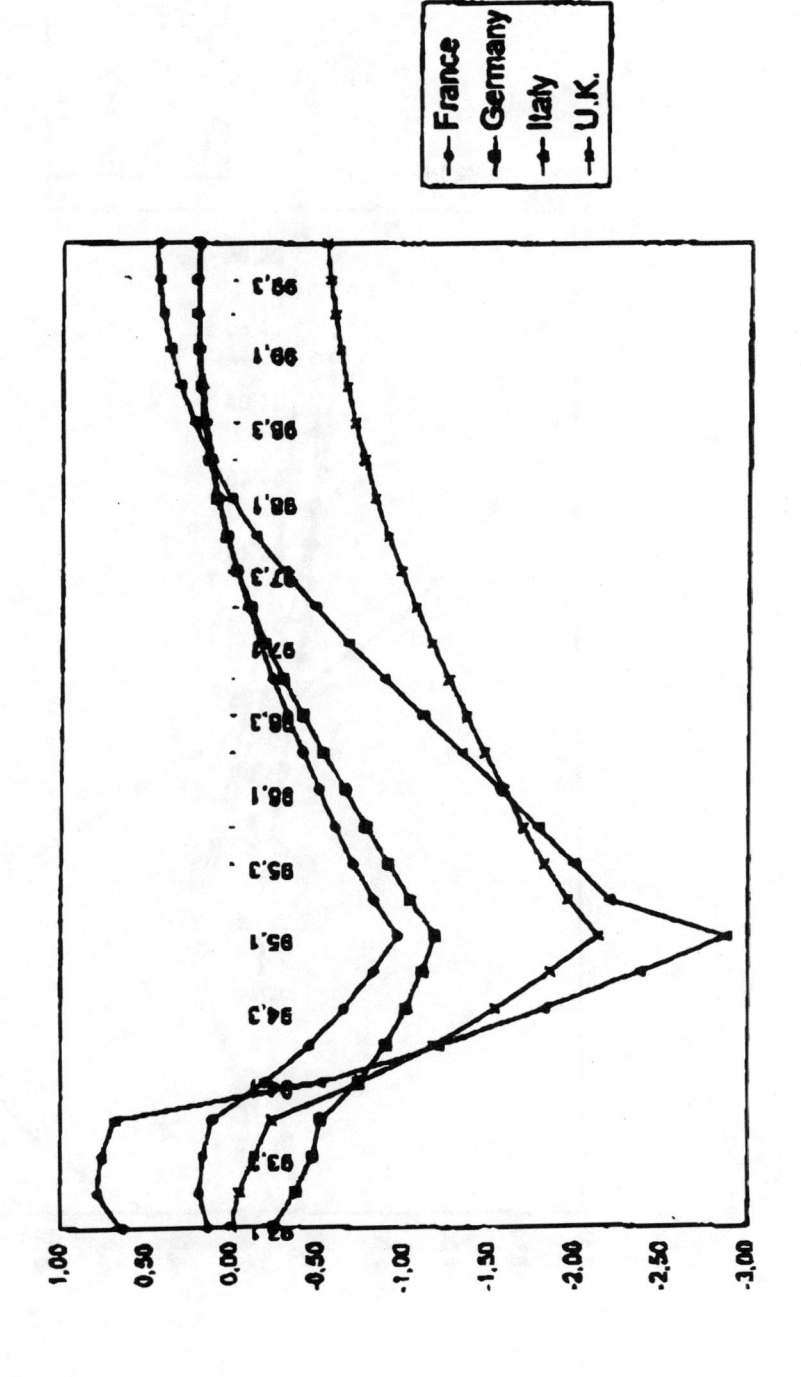

Figure 1

Real GDP, Flexible Exchange Rates
(Percentage deviations from baseline)

Figure 2
Real GDP, Fixed ERM Exchange Rates
(Percentage deviations from baseline)

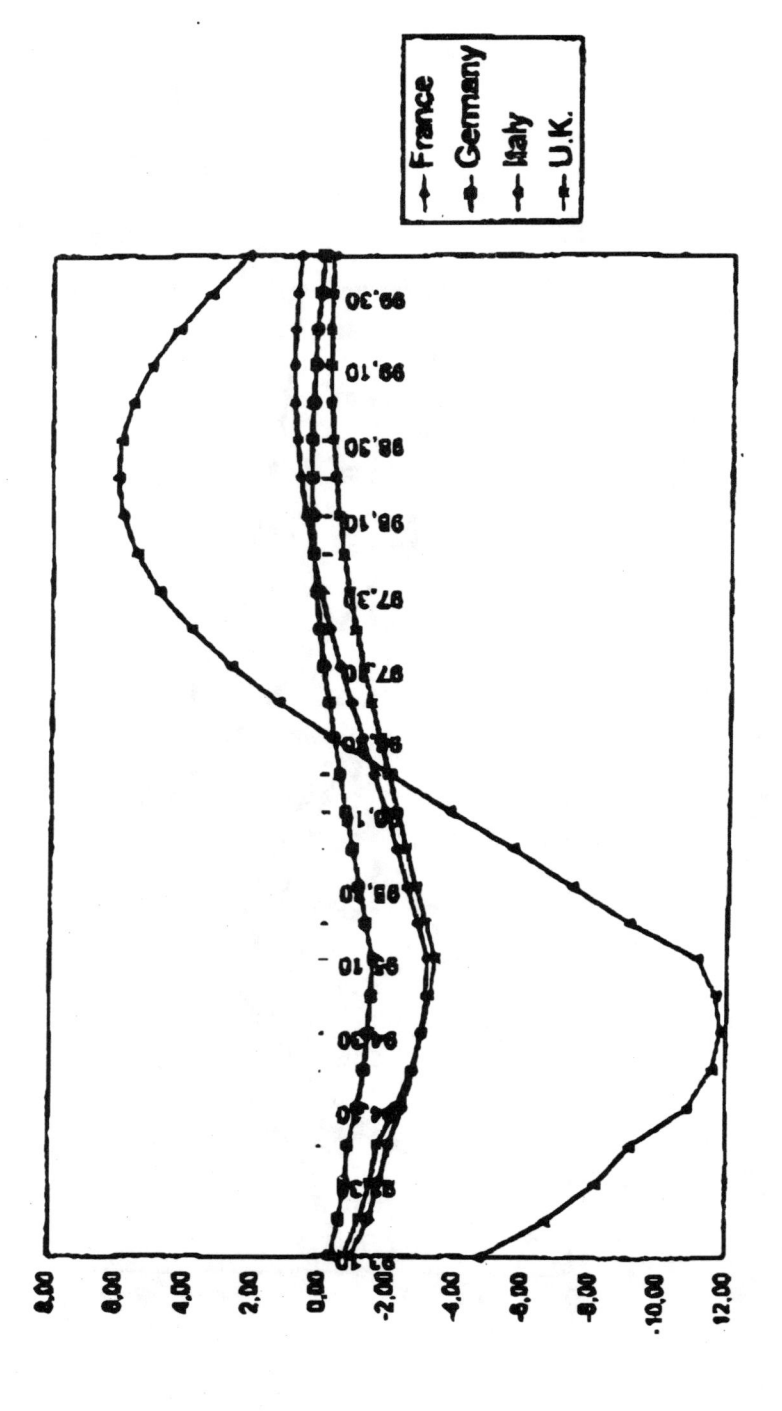

to monetary union. (The convergence criteria specified in the protocol to the Maastricht Treaty require countries qualifying for participation in Stage III not just to meet the debt and deficit criteria, but also to hold their exchange rates stable without involuntary realignments or excessive tensions for at least two years and to maintain interest rates and inflation rates close to those of the best performing EU member states.)

All European economies are struck by recessions. Figure 1 shows the movement of output under flexible exchange rates. Reflecting expectational effects, the German and UK recessions begin even before the actual cuts set in. The recessions deepen for two years; the deepest one occurs in Italy and the least significant one in France. Recovery commences after two years, with output continuing to rise through the end of the simulation. Except in the UK, where output remains below the baseline throughout, recovery raises output above baseline levels in the fifth year. Post-recession expansions are modest: in each country there is a net output loss over the cycle.

Because the fiscal criteria target deficit/GDP ratios, not deficits themselves, public spending must fall by more than the initial percentage specified when the program begins. (If the criteria require spending cuts of 3 percent of GDP at the starting point and output falls by 10 percent on impact in the subsequent recession, for example, spending must be cut even further to meet the targeted ratio of spending to GDP.) This further deepens the recession, which in turn amplifies the need for fiscal retrenchment and magnifies the multiplier effects of the fiscal contraction.

Figure 2 shows that the recessions are deeper and more prolonged under fixed than flexible exchange rates. The fixed rates of the EMS cause deeper recessions because they prevent interest rates outside Germany from falling and because they remove the stabilizing real-exchange rate adjustment that occurs under flexible rates. The contrast illustrates the value of external flexibility in a period when countries need to adjust differentially to the fiscal criteria of the Maastricht Treaty and suggests that maintaining fixed rates is not desirable in the final stages of the transition to monetary union.

In a continent just emerging from its worst recession in fifty years, this recessionary outcome is something policymakers are understandably reluctant to risk. Strict application of the fiscal criteria is therefore unlikely. As Stage III approaches, countries aspiring to participate in EMU will point to the excessive cost of meeting the fiscal conditions. France may then be let in as a political necessity, but what about Belgium? And if Belgium is let in, what about Italy? Clearly it will be hard to justify decisions that discriminate between states with similar debts and deficits. The result will be a political bargain over membership in which numerical guidelines play no role.

Nor are binding debt and deficit limits sensible devices for encouraging the pursuit of sound fiscal policies in Stage III. EMU will tie each national government's monetary hand behind its back, leaving it unable to tailor interest rates to domestic conditions. To also immobilize its fiscal hand and neutralize the operation of its automatic stabilizers would leave its economy defenseless in the face of macroeconomic fluctuations.

But to disregard German concern over fiscal policy would doom the prospects for EMU. There will be no monetary union without Germany, and Germany will not participate without reassurance. Germany's finance minister Theo Waigel recently tabled a proposal for a stability pact among EMU countries. Waigel would commit them to run deficits not exceeding 1 percent of GDP in normal times, require a deposit of 0.25 percent GDP from countries violating the 3 percent limit, and create an EU stability council to monitor compliance and issue guidelines for fiscal policy.

Unfortunately, there is little hope that a European Union already plagued by its inability to force members to abide by the rules of the Single Market could actually collect substantial fines. Fining a government with a revenue shortfall would only widen its deficit. When deciding whether to impose a fine, the stability council would likely seek to determine whether the deficit is due to a revenue shortfall caused by cyclical conditions or to excessive spending. This would invite political haggling and rob the process of credibility.

The solution is not stricter application of arbitrary indicators and penalties but reform of the procedures by which national fiscal policies are made. Study after study (e.g., von Hagen and Harden 1994; Alesina et al. 1995) have shown that budgetary procedures that limit free-riding behavior are conducive to sound fiscal outcomes. "Good" procedures include agenda-setting power for the finance minister, an annual fiscal round beginning with a binding vote on the overall size of the budget, strict limits on the legislature's power to increase spending in-year, and a prohibition of supplementary budgets. An annual budget round that begins with a binding vote on the overall size of the budget forces special interests to negotiate difficult compromises, limiting deficit bias. More agenda-setting power for the finance minister and a line-item veto similarly reduce the bias toward excessive deficits produced by fractionalized parliaments. Nations that follow such procedures run smaller deficits and accumulate smaller debts.

More drastic reform would establish in each country a national debt board responsible for setting a binding ceiling on the annual increase in public debt and with the power to enforce it. A binding limit would force special interests to acknowledge the existence of a global budget constraint and to agree to difficult compromises. The debt board would be politically independent of the government. Its members would be appointed to long terms in office. Their mandate would be to safeguard the soundness of the public finances and, without compromising that priority, to foster the general economic policies of the government.

This approach is consistent with that adopted to guide the policies of the ECB. The framers of the Maastricht Treaty were not so silly as to set arbitrary numerical targets for money growth. Rather, they gave the ECB a mandate to pursue price stability and specified the procedures it was to follow. They made sure that its executive board was independent, that its members would serve long terms in office, and that they would not take advice from national governments. Similarly constituted national debt boards could adopt a long-term perspective on fiscal policy. They could authorize budget deficits in recessions but offset these with surpluses subsequently. Political bias toward excessive deficits would be eliminated without placing fiscal policymakers in a straitjacket.

National debt boards would be preferable to the stability council proposed by Mr. Waigel. A stability council would make national fiscal policies the subject of international political bargains. European governments are hardly known for delivering impartial judgments on one another's compliance with EU rules —witness their notorious trading of exceptions in state aids and subsidies. National debt boards, in contrast, would rely on national enforcement and on the intimate knowledge of their members of the domestic fiscal situation. In this as in other senses, they would be consistent with the principle of subsidiarity. If Germany needs reassurance, other member-states can provide it by reforming their budgetary procedures along these lines.

The current debate points ineluctably to one of two outcomes: no EMU or macroeconomic disaster. Modest procedural reform—or if that is judged inadequate, the establishment of national debt boards—offers a third alternative that can reconcile Germany's desire for sound fiscal policy with Europe's need for macroeconomic flexibility. This approach could be adopted without any rewriting of the Maastricht Treaty itself. States are already obligated to see that their budgetary procedures enable them to comply with the provisions of the treaty. It would therefore suffice to agree at the 1996 Intergovernmental Conference that the Council should evaluate budgetary procedures—as opposed to merely budgetary outturns—as part of its judgment in 1998 about which states fulfill the conditions for the adoption of the single currency. If this approach is taken by the Intergovernmental Conference, EMU is still possible.

REFERENCES

Alesina, Alberto, Ricardo Hausmann, Rudolf Hommes, and Ernesto Stein. 1995. "Budget Institutions and Fiscal Performance in Latin America." Unpublished manuscript, Interamerican Development Bank.

Eichengreen, Barry, and Jürgen von Hagen. 1995. "Fiscal Restrictions and Monetary Union: Rationales, Repercussions, Reforms." *Empirica* (forthcoming).

von Hagen, Jürgen, and Ian J. Harden. 1994. "National Budget Processes and Fiscal Performance." *European Economy Reports and Studies* 3: 311–408.

von Hagen, Jürgen, and Stephan Lutz. 1995. "Monetary and Fiscal Policies on the Way to EMU." Working paper, University of Mannheim.

Taylor, John B. 1993. *Macroeconomic Policy in a World Economy*. New York: Norton.

ECONOMIC COHESION IN AN ENLARGED EUROPEAN UNION

Manuel Porto

EVOLUTION OF EU REGIONAL POLICY

Before we analyze the implications of eastern enlargement in the European Union (EU) it may perhaps be worthwhile to summarize the history of regional policy in the EU and the reasons behind it. In the founding treaty—i.e., the Treaty of Rome—regional policy enjoyed neither an article nor a title, much less a mechanism.* Thereafter, the evolution that took place was nothing short of remarkable: creation of the General Directorate for Regional Development (DG 16) in 1968; creation of the European Regional Development Fund (ERDF) in 1975; inclusion of regional policy in the treaty through the Single Act in 1986; and revision of the regulations in 1988. Moreover, the increasing importance of regional policy is clear from the increases in its funding. Between 1975 and 1988 ERDF funds increased from 257.6 to 3,684.0 million ECUs (from a share of 4.8 to a share of 8.1 percent of the Community budget). From 1989 to 1993, with the first budgetary perspectives, the total amount allocated to the structural funds was doubled. With the current budgetary perspectives (including the new Cohesion Fund) it will increase from 22,129 million ECUs in 1993 to 31,770 million in 1999—from a share of 28.6 to a share of 36.0 percent of the EU budget (doubling once more for the "cohesion" countries: Greece, Portugal, Spain, and Ireland).

What factors explain this evolution, which is unparalleled in any other policy area? One important factor was a sharper awareness of, and an increase in, regional inequalities. In the beginning only Italy

---

*Only in the preamble and in Article 2 were passing references made to more equilibrium, and in Article 92 regional development was admitted as an exception to the ban on public subsidies.

70   Manuel Porto

had a serious internal imbalance, but this situation changed markedly with the entry of some of the new members—namely, Ireland, Greece, Portugal, and Spain. Moreover, the greater attention to regional policy was due to a deeper understanding of the cost of regional disparities: in addition to social and political reasons, it was increasingly recognized that they were economically harmful for the whole Community. Regional disparities cause external diseconomies in some congested areas and jeopardize the opportunity for a more efficient use of the resources available, some of them in less favored regions.

RESULTS ACHIEVED

The full effect of a structural policy can be correctly known only some years later, when the economic and social effects resulting from improvements in a country's capacity can be measured.[1] But it can be anticipated that they are substantial in Europe if we bear in mind the amounts allocated as a percentage of GDP and of investment (Table 1), as well as the nature of the improvements made in basic infrastructures, R&D, or professional training. It is estimated that

Table 1

Funds of the First Community Support Framework

Country	Percentage of GDP (Annual average: 1989–93)	Percentage of Investment (1992)
Greece	2.9%	13.9%
Ireland	2.2	12.7
Portugal	3.4	11.1
Spain	0.5	2.4

these funds contributed to additional increases in GDP (in Spain and Italy in their objective 1 regions); see Table 2. With the rates of GDP growth shown in Table 2, there was an approximation between the four less developed countries and the EU average (Table 3). We can see that only Greece did not recover. With the other three and with all four there was an approximation (which was, however, interrupted in the 1990s, as will be noted below).

Table 2

GDP Growth, 1989–93
(*Annual average*)

Country	Total	Without the Funds	Additional Increase
Greece	1.6	1.1	0.5
Ireland	4.0	3.5	0.5
Portugal	4.1	3.4	0.7
Spain (obj. 1)	3.5	3.4	0.3
Italy (obj. 1)	2.6	2.4	0.3

Table 3

Approximation of Growth in Greece, Portugal, Ireland, and Spain with EU Average

Year	Greece	Portugal	Ireland	Spain	EU-15
1986	61.4	53.9	61.3	69.9	100
1990	58.9	59.6	70.8	74.3	100
1995	60.0	67.9	85.3	76.1	100

Source: European Commission, DG-II, *Statistical Annex of European Economy,* June 1995.

THE PATH TOWARD ECONOMIC AND MONETARY UNION

We can expect that the opportunities of the single market and the introduction of the single currency, leading to higher rates of growth, will contribute to more equilibrium in the EU.[2] It has been so in the past: more equilibrium between the beginning and 1973, when the rate of growth was quite high; an increase of the imbalance between 1973 and 1985, when some recession took place; and some approximation among countries since then, when the economies once again had higher rates of growth.[3] In particular it can be expected that the benefits of the single currency will be more tangible in the less advanced economies, where the costs of uncertainty and instability are higher.[4] Of course, they will also be especially high in more open economies, as is the case of the Portuguese economy. If it is so, is it not a question of just waiting for this favorable evolution? If not, some intervention should take place.

First, attention must be given to the fact that the convergence registered among countries has not been mirrored in convergence among regions. According to the data of the fourth report on regional policy (European Commission 1991: 87), from 1980 to 1988 there was neither approximation among the twenty-five more developed regions and the twenty-five less developed regions, nor among the ten more and the ten less developed regions of the EU (NUTs 2). In Portugal, taking into account data until 1991, we can see that there was no approximation between two Portuguese regions and the EU average (Table 4). While the Lisbon, the Northern, and the Algarve regions registered an approximation to the EU average (the Lisbon region reached 82 percent), the situation of the Central Region was not improved, and there was deterioration of the relative situation in the Alentejo Region.

Even general approximation among countries has been slow. According to Grahl and Teague (1990, using Commission data), with 1988 as the first year, in order to have a GDP per capita corresponding to 90 percent of the EU average by the year 2007, Portugal would

Table 4

GDP Per Capita
(Percent of EU average)

Area	1980	1991
Continental Portugal	53%	60%
Northern Region	44	54
Central Region	42	42
Lisbon and Vale do Tejo Region	69	82
Alentejo Region	49	36
Algarve Region	48	52

Source: Instituto Nacional de Estatística and European Commission, *Eurostat.* Using different criteria, research by the Direcção Geral do Desenvolvimento Regional shows quite different results, with a clear reduction of the Portuguese imbalance. This is indeed a surprising result, which cannot explain the enormous movement of people that occurred during the decade (between 1981 and 1991) from the interior to metropolitan areas (see Porto 1996).

have to register yearly growth rates 2.6 percent higher than the EU average—clearly an unrealistic target.

The difficulty of catching up with the other countries is nowadays further increased by the need to fulfill the criteria of nominal convergence established in Maastricht. Since the less developed countries generally suffer higher levels of inflation, interest rates, budgetary deficit, and public deficit, the effort they must make is much more difficult for them than for the more developed countries of the EU. It is precisely the less developed countries which will be forced to follow more restrictionist policies, and this will delay their development. In fact, these policies, following the recession at the beginning of the 1990s, are causing special difficulties in some of these countries (Table 5, including forecasts). With the exception of Ireland, the difficulties of the other three countries are quite clear, mainly between 1992 and 1994, but in 1996 they again had higher rates of growth than the whole of the EU.

To help the effort of Greece, Portugal, Ireland, and Spain, the countries with GDP per capita below 90 percent of the EU average, the Cohesion Fund was created.* With the existing difficulties in mind,

Table 5

Annual Growth in GDP

Country	1990	1991	1992	1993	1994	1995	1996	1997
Greece	-0.1	3.2	-0.8	-0.5	1.1	1.6	1.9	2.2
Spain	3.7	2.2	-0.7	-1.1	2.0	3.1	2.9	3.2
Ireland	8.6	2.9	5.0	4.0	6.3	6.9	5.6	4.8
Portugal	4.3	2.1	1.1	-1.2	1.1	3.0	3.7	3.3
EU-15[a]	1.2	1.4	1.6	1.2	3.2	2.1	2.6	2.9

Source: European Commission, DG-II, *Statistical Annex of European Economy,* June 1995.

[a]Not including five *Länder* of the Federal Republic of Germany.

*With the Cohesion Fund trans-European transport networks and environmental investments can be financed.

the principle of additionality was not applied, and EU participation was allowed to go up to 85 percent of the total. But according to the Maastricht requirements, the money is available only if the countries have a program to fulfill the criteria of nominal convergence—in other words, if they follow a policy which delays real convergence.

There are reasons, therefore, to continue and even to reinforce the regional policy of the EU, just as steps are being taken for the introduction of the single currency. Here it should be stressed that greater spatial balance is not only for the benefit of the less developed countries and regions. It is a basic prerequisite for the success of the common currency. In particular, it is necessary to avoid the risk that "disparities within the Community would cause persistent capital and labour flows from the less prosperous to the richer regions, creating both economic and political tensions that could put the whole process in jeopardy" (Britton and Mayes 1992: 65).

FORTHCOMING ENLARGEMENT

The enlargement now foreseen of ten Central and East European countries is to a large extent for political reasons, as a way to assure stability to countries which were ruled for many years by Communist dictatorships.[*] In addition, it is of course expected that enlargement will enable the EU to become an even stronger economic area, with increased market opportunities, thereby reinforcing its position as the largest economic bloc in the world, ahead of NAFTA. However, we must be aware of the difficulties of the intermediate period, which may last for some years.[†] First, Central and East European countries have lived for a long time with a quite different economic system; time is therefore required for them to fully adapt to the mechanisms of a market economy. Moreover, particular difficulties arise in two areas, agriculture and regional development.[**]

[*]Malta and Cyprus are also part of the expansion plans, but in their case economic difficulties do not arise.

[†]For Spain and Portugal, whose economies were more similar to those of the countries which were already members of the EEC, there was a nine-year gap between the request for negotiations, in 1977, and adhesion in 1986.

[**]Despite the existing differences in wage levels, it is not expected that unsolvable problems will arise with the free movement of people to EU countries.

In agriculture enormous difficulties arise as a result of the existing differences in prices and production in these countries. The application of the present Common Agricultural Policy (CAP) would have unacceptable repercussions on the standard of living of the people and on the EU budget. People with much lower wages could not afford the "European" prices, and to maintain the guarantee system of the EAGGF, the budget would need, according to Anderson and Tyers (1993), 37.6 billion ECUs more for just the four Višegrad countries. That is, for these countries alone, it would be necessary to spend more than the total amount spent in 1993: 36.7 billion.*

According to Baldwin (1994: 190–92) the movement from the four Višegrad countries (Poland, Czech Republic, Slovakia, and Hungary) will be of between 3.2 and 6.4 million people toward a space with about 370 million. Only local problems will arise if the settlement of these people takes place in overcrowded metropolitan areas of two or three countries. In this analysis it is perhaps worthwhile to recall the Portuguese experience on emigration. In the 1960s and 1970s, when the country was not a member and integration was legally difficult, more than one million people emigrated to EEC countries. However, a large movement has not taken place since Portugal's integration because of the improvement of economic conditions in the country (although wages are still much lower) and indeed as a result nowadays of a much lower demand (pull effect) from the main countries of Europe (i.e., France and Germany), which have high levels of unemployment.

*Enormous social and reconversion problems must be solved given the big share of the work force still in agriculture in most of these countries:

Agricultural Sector in Central and Eastern Europe

Country	Percent of GDP	Percent of Employment
Estonia	10.4%	8.2%
Latvia	10.6	18.4
Lithuania	11.0	22.4
Poland	6.3	25.6
Czech Republic	3.3	5.6
Slovakia	5.8	8.1
Hungary	6.4	10.1
Romania	20.2	35.2
Bulgaria	10.0	21.2
Slovenia	4.9	10.7
CE-10	7.8	26.7
EU-15	2.5	5.7

Source: European Commission, DG-II and DG-VI.

Note: There is a big difference relative to the EU, with a much higher share of active population in agriculture living with much lower standards (only the four Višegrad countries have the present agricultural population of the EU).

This problem cannot be solved through transfers from other categories of the present budget. Agricultural and structural actions (which will be mentioned below) account for 81.4 percent of the 1996 budget, so only 18.6 percent remains for all the other categories. Some are essential policies and expenditures (internal and external policies and administration) which cannot be reduced. In any case the amounts would not be enough for CAP needs. (Their 1996 total was just 13.5 billion ECUs.) Moreover, it would not make sense to expand one policy (the CAP) with so many internal costs: for the citizens as consumers, for the entrepreneurs transforming more expensive agricultural raw materials, and for the budget (still 47.9 percent of the total in 1996). It is also an unfair policy, benefiting mainly some rich countries and rich farmers, and one which makes the international negotiations of the EU more difficult, forcing it to compromise in sectors in which it has good export capacities and employs an important share of the labor force.*

With the adhesion of new members different hypotheses have been considered, including that of having two separate regimes: the existing CAP would be applied to the present members and another agricultural policy (or no policy at all) to the new members. However, it would be a totally unacceptable solution for economic and political reasons.[5] As has been pointed out by various authors and politicians, the only way out will be an important new reform of the agricultural policy, along the lines of the 1992 reform, allowing prices closer to those on the world market, together with a reinforcement of direct aid to less-well-off people and to the reconversion of rural areas.[6]

The need to apply EU regional policy to the new members is justified by their present level of development (and of course their development prospects), with GDP per capita below the EU average (Table 6).

---

*In 1993 23.4 percent of the total went to France (with a GDP per capita of 112, over the EU base), 14.2 percent to Germany (101.7), 14 percent to Italy (104.0), and 12.1 percent to Spain (77.2); 1.4 percent went to Portugal. According to the Commission, 80 percent of the EAGGF funds go to the twenty richest farmers of the EU.

Table 6

GDP per Capita (1993)
(PPS)

Country	ECU per Capita	Percent of EU
Estonia	6,236	38.4%
Latvia	4,593	28.7
Lithuania	2,828	17.7
Poland	5,029	31.5
Czech Republic	6,738	42.2
Slovakia	5,365	33.6
Hungary	5,720	35.8
Romania	2,669	15.7
Bulgaria	5,280	33.0
Slovenia	8,076	50.5
Greece	9,998	52.6
Ireland	12,826	68.1
Portugal	10,935	57.1
Spain	12,330	79.1
EU-12	15,835	100.0

Source: DG-II and DG-VI, based on data of the World Bank.

Note: The Economist (1995: 87–88) gives worse figures (not with PPS values): 2,080 for Lithuania; 3,420 for Poland; 4,920 for the Czech Republic; 3,390 for Slovakia; 4,690 for Hungary; 1,565 for Romania; and 1,460 for Bulgaria.

According to present criteria, all these countries are in principle objective 1 regions (despite the fact that with their integration, 75 percent of GDP will correspond to quite a lower level); thus enormous budgetary difficulties will arise. According to an evaluation made for the European Commission (1993), the four Višegrad countries alone would get 26 billion ECUs (more than the total amount spent on members in 1993 of 22.19 billion).* These amounts are nonetheless well below those needed for the agricultural policy to improve the overall conditions of the EU. The positive rates of growth estimated and foreseen for these countries give us some reason for optimism. For 1995 and 1996 these values are shown in Table 7. However, for these countries it will be a long haul before they come close to the EU average. In an evaluation similar to the one made by Grahl and Teague for the cohesion countries (1990), with the assumption that the EU would grow 2 percent per annum, calculations determined the number of years the new members would need to reach 75 percent of the present EU level (Table 8). Of course, as noted, their accession will bring the 75 percent target to a much lower level. In any case, it will be long and difficult for them, and it is not certain that they will be able to maintain even slightly higher rates of growth.

---

*The dimension of the difficulties is of course also connected with the population and area of the countries, which can be compared with the EU-15:

Country	Population (Millions)	Area (Millions of hectares)
Estonia	1.5	4.5
Latvia	2.6	6.5
Lithuania	3.7	6.5
Poland	38.4	31.3
Czech Republic	10.3	7.9
Slovakia	5.3	4.9
Hungary	10.3	9.2
Romania	22.8	23.8
Bulgaria	8.5	11.1
Slovenia	2.0	2.0
CE-10	105.5	107.7
EU-15	369.9	327.4

Source: DG-II and DG-VI.

Note: It would therefore be an increase of 28.5 percent in the population and 32.9 percent of the present area.

Table 7

GDP Growth Rates

Country	1995	1996
Estonia	5.0	4.0
Latvia	1.0	3.0
Lithuania	3.0	3.5
Poland	5.9	4.8
Czech Republic	3.8	4.2
Slovakia	5.6	4.6
Hungary	1.5	3.0
Romania	4.0	4.0
Bulgaria	2.0	3.0

Source: The Economist (1995: 87–88).

Table 8

Years for the Višegrad Group and Slovenia to Catch Up to 75 Percent of EU-12 Average Income

Country	3% Growth	4% Growth	6% Growth
Czech Republic	28	21	14
Hungary	35	26	18
Slovakia	51	39	26
Poland	44	33	22
Višegrad-4 average	40	30	20
Slovenia	15	11	8

Source: Baldwin (1994: 168).

INSUFFICIENCY OF BUDGETARY RESOURCES

The budget of the EU currently represents a mere 1.23 percent of total GDP. (It will represent 1.27 percent in 1999.) One cannot therefore compare this budget with that of a federal state. Indeed it should not be compared, given the quite different political nature of the EU, not to mention the fact that the Maastricht Treaty has reinforced the subsidiarity principle.[7] But even in the correct political and economic framework, some change must take place if we want to welcome new members without harming the integration process.

As stressed above, the amounts of the other categories cannot be reduced, and in no case would they be enough to cover the agricultural and regional policies. Even with a new reform of the CAP, important amounts will be needed for income maintenance and rural development, not only in the present member-states, but also to a greater extent in new member-states. Moreover, substantial amounts must be allocated to regional promotion (and to other structural improvements). Present members, which continue to require greater cohesion, must avoid the risk of being harmed in the process of integration. Of course the requirements will be sharply increased with enlargement.

There is therefore a tradeoff between widening and deepening if the EU's budget remains at the present level. Preference must indeed be given to deepening, in the interest of third world countries as well, because a strong Europe enhances their development process. If governments want to maintain the present budgetary level, they should state very clearly that an enlargement is not foreseen in the immediate future. This is an acceptable option, as it can be accompanied by a policy of closer cooperation with the candidates—i.e., exploring to a greater extent the opportunities offered by the agreements already reached. It is even possible that this will be a more favorable solution for the candidates, who would then not be forced to accept all EU rules.

If, however, it is decided that enlargement will take place during the coming budgetary perspectives, there is no alternative to an increase in the budget. In the Delors II package (COM [92] 200) an increase of up to 1.37 percent of the GDP in 1999 was suggested, but the governments did not agree to it. Now there is no alternative: the government cannot decide on enlargement without accepting some increase.

With an increased budget more attention must be given to the resources, and the present regressive distribution must be avoided (Table 9).[8]

The Netherlands and Belgium are special cases, owing to the great amount of goods which are imported through Amsterdam and

Table 9

Own Resources/GDP per Capita, 1993

Country		Country	
Belgium	1.45	Italy	0.99
Denmark	1.09	Luxembourg	1.13
France	1.11	Netherlands	1.59
Germany	1.18	Portugal	1.40
Greece	1.37	Spain	1.14
Ireland	1.49	United Kingdom	0.87

Source: Coget (1994: 83; see also figure on p. 67).

Antwerp and taxed with the common tariff and the agricultural levies but are then transported to other countries (in particular Germany). Besides these cases, it can be noted (for example) that an Irish citizen pays 1.49 percent of his income for the EU budget, a Portuguese, 1.40, and a Greek 1.37, while a German pays 1.18, a Dane 1.09, and a Briton 0.87.* In a "citizens'" Europe, in which people should consider themselves responsible participants, this is an unacceptable situation.† A proportional (or even progressive) distribution must be reached, with the greater participation of the Fourth Resource (GNP percentage) or perhaps a proportional participation of the income tax of the citizens.

Of course, the present situation of inequity would be aggravated with the Central and East European countries, where people have lower living standards. Their foreseen integration is therefore

---

*This is as a result of the role of the three forms of indirect taxation (VAT percentage, customs duties, and agricultural levies), with a regressive distribution, not compensated by the GNP contribution. (In 1994 they represented 72.7 percent of the total.)

†Aggravated by the inequity of the distribution of the funds of the CAP, mentioned above. It remains, despite the improvement following the 1992 reform. (For Portugal there was an increase in the participation of the EAGGF from 0.6 percent in 1986 to 1.4 percent of the total in 1994; see Leygues 1994a: 24 and 1994b.)

an additional reason for a quick reform of the EU's own resources, which cannot remain with a regressive distribution.*

NOTES

1. We have seen this difficulty in Porto (1991 and 1996).

2. On results expected, see *European Economy*, nos. 35 and 44.

3. See European Commission (1991: 19) and Abraham and Rompuy (1992), who point out some reasons for this interconnection.

4. On these expected spatial benefits of the single currency, see Ch. 4 of *European Economy*, no. 44, and Porto (1993). In the United States, which has had a single currency for many years, regional imbalances are much smaller than in the EU (see Boltho 1994).

5. Even institutionally, as Baldwin (1994) stresses, "we would have the unacceptable situation of second-class passengers voting for the deterioration of the conditions of the first-class passengers."

6. The 1992 reform was achieved during the Portuguese presidency. On its effects see Ockenden and Franklin (1995), suggesting the strategy to be followed in the coming enlargement. See also Cunha (1995); European Parliament (1995); and European Commission (1995).

7. In particular the suggestion of the McDougall Report (European Commission 1977) of a budget corresponding to 5–7 percent of total GDP cannot be accepted.

8. Baldwin (1994: 163) says that "the EU budget is progressive in that it transfers resources to the poorer countries." However, in addition to "some anomalies"—such as the fact that Denmark and Luxembourg are net recipients (see Franklin 1992)—regressivity, as a measure of equity, makes sense only if we take into account people's income, not the income of territories.

---

*Their situation would be aggravated with the foreseen introduction of a CO^2 tax; poorer families must spend a higher share of their income on energy, and an outdated industry requires much higher shares of energy spending. Moreover, energy taxation would create a much higher burden for peripheral countries, which depend on a greater extent on imports from and exports to the countries of the center (the richer countries).

REFERENCES

Abraham, Philip, and Van Rompuy, Paul. 1992. "Convergence-Divergence and the Implications for Community Structural Policies." Catholic University of Louven. CES research paper.

Anderson, Kim, and Tyers, R. 1993. "Implications of EC Expansion for European Agricultural Policies, Trade and Welfare." CEPR Discussion Paper No. 829.

Baldwin, Richard. 1994. *Towards an Integrated Europe*. London: Centre for Economic Policy Research (CEPR).

Boltho, Andrea. 1994. "A Comparison of Regional Differentials in the European Community and the United States." In *Improving Economic and Social Cohesion in the European Community*, ed. Jorgen Moreonsen. Basingstoke: Macmillan, pp. 41-53.

Britton, Andrew, and Mayes, David. 1992. *Achieving Union in Europe*. London: Sage Publications.

Coget, Gérard. 1994. "Les Resources propres communautaires." *Revue française de finances publiques*, no. 45: 51-96.

Cunha, Arlindo. 1995. "A agricultura europeia na encruzilhada." *Expresso*, 14 April.

The Economist. 1995. *The World in 1996*. London.

European Commission. 1977. *Report of the Study Group on the Role of Public Finance in European Integration* (MacDougall Report). Brussels.

―――――. 1991. *The Regions in the 1990's: Fourth Periodic Report on the Social and Economic Situation and Development of the Regions of the Community*. Brussels and Luxembourg.

―――――. 1995. *Study on Alternative Strategies for the Development of Relations in the Field of Agriculture between the EU and the Associated Countries with a View to Future Accession of These Countries*. Agricultural Strategy Paper (COM [95] 607).

European Parliament. 1995. Directorate General for Research, *Agricultural Strategies for the Enlargement of the EU to Central and Eastern European Countries: Critical Review of Four Studies Ordered by the Commission of the European Community*; A. Buckwell, J. Haynes, S. Danidova, and A. Kwiecinski, *Feasibility of an Agricultural Strategy to Prepare the Countries of Central and Eastern Europe for EU Accession*; L. P. Mahé, J. Cordier, H. Guyomard, and T. Roe, *L'Agriculture et l'élargissement de l'Union Européenne aux pays d'Europe Centrale et Orientale: Transition en vue de l'intégration pour la transition?*; S. Tangermann, T. E. Josling, and W. Munch, *Pre-Accession Agricultural Policies for Central Europe and the European Union*; and S. Tarditi, S. Senior-Nello, J. Marsh, G. Blaas, L. Kelly, A. Nucifor, H. Thiele, and A. Bastiani, *Agricultural Strategies for the Enlargement of the European Union to Central and Eastern European Countries*.

Franklin, M. 1992. "The EC Budget: Realism, Redistribution and Radical Reform." London: Royal Institute of International Affairs. Discussion Paper No. 42.

Graal, John, and Teague, Paul. 1990–92. *The Big Market: The Future of the European Community*. London: Lawrence and Wizhart.

Kramer, Heinz. 1993. "The European Community's Response to the 'New Eastern Europe.'" *Journal of Common Market Studies* 31, 2: 213–44.

Leygues, Jean-Charles. 1994a. *Les Politiques internes de l'Union Européenne*. Paris: Librairie Génerale de Droit et de Jurisprudence.

—————. 1994b. "Evaluation des politiques internes communautaires et de leurs dépenses." *Revue française de finances publiques*, no. 45: 97–164.

Ockenden, Jonathan, and Franklin, Michael. 1995. *European Agriculture: Making the CAP Fit the Future*. London: Pinter.

Porto, Manuel. 1991. "European Integration and Regional Development Policy in Portugal." In *Issues in Contemporary Economics*, vol. 2: *Macroeconomics and Econometrics*, ed. Marc Nerlove, pp. 183–210. Basingstoke: Macmillan (in association with the International Economic Association).

—————. 1993. "A dimensão especial da União Europeia." In Curso de Estudos Europeus da Faculdade de Direito, *A União Europeia*, pp. 61–89. Coimbra.

—————. 1996. "O ordenamento do território face aos desafios da competitividade." In Instituto de Estudos Geográficos da Faculdade de Letras, *Dinamismo sócio-económico e re-organização territorial: Processo de urbanização e de reestruturação produtiva*. Coimbra.

SOME REFLECTIONS ON THE PROBLEM OF DIFFERENTIATION: THE CASE OF PORTUGAL

Paulo de Pitta e Cunha

The problem of differentiation, which was in the past of minor relevance, now comes to the fore in the European Union (EU). This appears in the form of either a potential conflict between large and small/medium countries (in regard mainly to population) or a confrontation in the future between full members of the economic and monetary union (EMU) and member-states with a derogation.

The first kind of opposition is becoming a serious question in the framework of prospective expansion. It is mainly reflected in the field of institutional reform. Small/medium states are concerned that their weight will diminish in the decision-making process of the EU. Large states are pushing for adjustments allowing for the maintenance or increase of their influence. It seems in regard to this question that small/medium states tend to become less federalist in their preference and more intergovernmentalist as they understand that the merger of sovereignties in a federal context may be detrimental to the preservation of their national identity.

The second kind of opposition is embodied in the conception of the EMU itself. Its first expression was the opting out granted to two member-states. Then, in the Maastricht Treaty, for the first time a central objective of integration was assumed to be pursued (albeit temporarily) by only a group of member-states. As no significant EMU is conceivable without the participation of Germany and France, the prospect of these large countries forming a "hard core" together with a few other member-states potentially creates the image of a "Directoire," with the exclusion of the majority of small/medium countries.

Let us examine how the problems of differentiation noted above can be seen to affect Portugal. Since Portugal is not a large country, the concern with the dilution of its relative influence and identity in a much wider EU implies a less euphoric endorsement of supranationalism by comparison with positions adopted in the recent past. It is unfortunate, however, that such concern is showing up only now, as it would have been wiser to try to moderate the integrationist impulse while the treaty was being negotiated. It would have been better for Portugal if real convergence had been included in the conditions for EMU, if an ineluctable timetable for the entry into the third stage had not been set up, and if the commitment to move to the third stage had been foreseen as a consequence of a separate decision by national governments and parliaments.

The issue of how far Portugal was prepared to go in the development of the political integration movement was never seriously considered. In my view, this discussion should have occurred *prior* to the commitment to enter the third stage, as the real reasons for the single currency seem to be closer to the design of establishing a European political power (sort of a European federation) than to the pragmatic logic of "one market, one currency." However, monetary union does not necessarily mean an irresistible drive toward a full federation. The heart of the problem lies in the methodology for decision-making in the second pillar of the Maastricht Treaty. Here the abandonment of the present unanimity rule would not be very far from the loss, for the individual member countries, of the attributes of sovereignty in international relations. But (hopefully) we are not yet there.

The convergence criteria and the automatic timetable for the third stage of EMU create a serious dilemma for Portugal. In order to avoid the discriminatory position of being left out of EMU and the inherent marginalization in the integration process, should Portugal employ all efforts to be in the front line of the third stage, even at the cost of real expansion and in the condition of productive sectors? Or would it be preferable for some years more to pursue flexible fiscal, monetary, and foreign exchange policies to achieve a more rapid real convergence—at the risk of being excluded from the core group of member-states of the EU and of facing an accrued vulnerability of the domestic currency?

Questions like these cannot be easily resolved. Many important factors that influence the costs and benefits of the choices are outside of Portugal's control. For example, if countries like Spain or Italy give up reaching the third stage by the automatic timetable, it will be easier for Portugal to adopt a similar position. If such a timetable is set aside and new, more flexible dates are fixed, the convergence effort will not be so drastic, as there will be more time to adjust. And so forth.

Thus far we have considered the (temporary) limitations on economic expansion resulting from the application of the convergence criteria for accession to the third stage of the EMU. A different question relates to the permanent features of the EMU.

The Maastricht Treaty focused much more on how to reach the third stage than on how the EMU, once established, would work. This leads to two problems. First, concern seems justified in regard to the possibility of a deflationary bias appearing in the EMU itself, once it is created. The mission of the supranational authorities charged with the definition of the monetary policy of the EU has been set up in a strict way in regard to the priority of monetary stability. The repression of excessive budgetary deficits is so severely pursued that a lack of dynamism in overall demand may in the future spread over the whole EU, with particularly serious consequences for the most fragile national economies.

Second, it is well known that the Maastricht path toward monetary union involves requirements of monetary and budgetary rigor, related to the view, underlying the treaty clauses on economic and monetary policy and its protocols, of a nominal convergence, not allowing in this regard for the setting up of conditions regarding real convergence. In this respect, the emphasis placed on social and economic cohesion seems somewhat precarious. This remains a problem, although the reduction of differences in development, to be achieved through structural funds, has been the object of specific rules, not contained in the central block of regulations concerning the creation of EMU.

It is true that the approval of the financing program corresponding to the Delors II package has been approved. But there is no certainty in regard to the renewal of the pledges beyond 1999. The Delors packages were negotiated and accepted by the main donors with a growing reluctance. Germany, for example, is apparently more interested in its eastern neighbors than in southern Europe. A link between the presence of the beneficiary countries in the third stage and a further effort in the area of cohesion is not guaranteed.

A more precise detailing of the future EMU should include instruments of compensation for asymmetric shocks and guarantees of support for real convergence through structural funds. This would be important to brighten the prospects of the participation of Portugal. At the same time, the regime of the countries which will not have fulfilled the convergence criteria in time to be in the front line has not been defined in the new regulations contained in the EC treaty.

The clarification of the relationship between such a group and the core is very important. It might contribute not only to diminishing the concern of member-states which have not yet achieved convergence, but also to setting aside the fears of the hard-core states in regard to competitive depreciations of the remaining currencies.

In the Green Paper of the Commission on the "Practical Arrangements for the Introduction of the Single Currency," in addition to the well-known arguments in favor of monetary integration—elimination of costs connected with the existence of several currencies, greater efficiency of the single market, etc.—it is stated that another advantage of the single currency will be "enhanced joint monetary sovereignty for the Member States." The argument here is that with the free movement of capital, an autonomous monetary policy is no longer possible. Therefore, a shared but effective responsibility over the common currency—a "joint monetary sovereignty"—is the best solution.

An identical reference to an enhanced joint sovereignty is usually presented as a justification, in other fields of integration, for the federal impulse. However, such a presentation corresponds to a rather euphemistic way of describing the cost of intense integration in terms of an effective deprivation of national powers.

If the relative importance that is still attributed to small and medium countries in the present EU of fifteen members is reduced in the future—and this seems to be an inescapable consequence of geographic expansion—then the influence of each member-state will have been diluted in such a way that instead of a "shared or enhanced sovereignty," the reality will more appropriately reflect a blunt loss of some of the still remaining national powers to the advantage of "federal" bodies. But here only a few large member-states still expect to retain a considerable part of their influence.

In the present stage of construction in the EU, the erosion of national identity through losses of sovereignty can no longer be considered a "theological question." Each member country should reflect on the very concept of a united Europe and on the role that the national states may expect to retain in the evolving union.

AGRICULTURE AND THE TRADE POLICY CHALLENGES FACING THE EUROPEAN UNION

Timothy Josling

The European Union (EU) faces a number of fundamental challenges to its trade and market policy in the coming decade. These challenges can be divided into those involving the internal market and the extension of this market to the countries of Central and Eastern Europe (CEEC), and those relating to external trade with other continents. Agricultural trade and domestic market policies are at the heart of both of these issues. This paper looks at the two sets of economic challenges and relates each to the issue of the development of agricultural policy in Europe, and in particular to the future course of the Common Agricultural Policy (CAP).

ENLARGEMENT AND THE INTERNAL MARKET

The most difficult challenge in the area of internal market policy for the EU in the next decade is how to absorb up to ten more countries.* These countries have low incomes at present—on average only 11 percent of the EU-15 average (see Table 1). But they have good potential for steady economic growth and high expectations on the part of their consumers. The workers in these countries are potentially mobile and will undoubtedly come looking for jobs if none are avail-

*Ten countries now have Association Agreements that are intended to lead up to membership. The Višegrad Four (the Czech Republic, Hungary, Poland, and Slovakia) along with Slovenia are considered to be the most ready for membership. Bulgaria, Romania, and the three Baltic countries (Estonia, Latvia, and Lithuania) are considered less likely to be prepared by the end of the decade. Malta and Cyprus have been promised entry negotiations as soon as the 1996 Intergovernmental Conference on institutional changes is over, presumably in 1997. Turkey is considered unlikely to be admitted as a full member, though a customs union with the EU is on the brink of being formed.

Agriculture & Trade Policy Challenges Facing the European Union   91

Table 1

Relative Size of CEEC-10 and EU-15

Variable	CEEC-10 (1)	EU-15 (2)	(1) as Percentage of (2)
Population (*Millions*)	105.5	369.7	29%
GDP (*Billions of ECU*)	188.3	5905.1	3
GDP per capita (*Thousands of ECU*)	1,786	15,972	11
Agricultural area (*Millions of hectares*)	60.6	138.1	44
Arable area (*Millions of hectares*)	42.3	77.1	55
Agricultural production (*Millions of ECU*)	14.7 (7.8%)	208.8 (2.5%)	7
Agricultural employment (*Thousands*)	9,540 (26%)	8,190 (5.7%)	130

Source: EU Commission.

able at home. The population in these ten countries is about 29 percent of that of the EU-15. Thus the challenge is to generate enough economic growth in these economies that they become sources of employment, a magnet for both domestic and foreign investment, and a buoyant market for goods from the EU-15. The danger is that they become a bottomless pit for public assistance in the form of programs and policies to support uneconomic industries, release workers in numbers enough to swamp EU-15 labor markets, and provide no offsetting economic benefits by purchasing "Western" goods. Such a development would threaten the foundations upon which the EU has been built, the single internal market, the free movement of labor and capital, the budgetary mechanism, and the common external policy, as well as the CAP and the Regional Fund.*

*There will also be a challenge to the monetary arrangements, including the adoption of a single currency, as well as to all the noneconomic policies and the institutions themselves.

PRESERVING THE SINGLE MARKET

The first aspect of this challenge is how to preserve the single market. The threat will be manifest through the pressure by producers in the present EU for relief from imports from the CEEC. "Sensitive" imports into the EU—including steel, textiles, and agricultural goods—are already controlled by quotas. The apprehension is not all in the existing EU. The corresponding fear in the prospective members is that of the demolition of entire industries in these countries by competition from the West. Everyone agrees that the markets must eventually be opened. The timing and sequencing is at issue.

The agricultural sector is in the thick of this debate. The single market for agricultural goods in the expanded EU is under threat. Those that would like to postpone the pressures on farmers in the current EU argue for a long transition. The new members would not get unlimited access to the markets in the West until producers in the West were able to withstand the competition. Thus the notion has been floated of a "green wall," with different price levels and policies each side of the wall. The political ramifications of such a two-tier agricultural policy are unclear. The economic costs of such a prolonged market segmentation are also difficult to calculate, as they depend on how the transition period is used. Those that argue for a more rapid docking of eastern and western agricultural markets seek to avoid the costs of a transition that merely postpones needed adjustments in the West. This would clarify the signal to the new members and help to prevent the construction of uneconomic agricultural sectors in those countries.

The Commission appears to be leaning toward the notion of a long transition period for the harmonization of agricultural prices. The argument seems to be based on the experience with the southern enlargement in 1986. This, however, begs the question of whether the analogy is closer to the Portuguese transition—a ten-year period designed to allow Portugal to adapt to Europe—or the Spanish case—a seven-year period for the EC to prepare for Spanish competition. Both adaptations are undoubtedly necessary in the case of eastern enlargement. The question is the balance between the two.

KEEPING LABOR MARKETS OPEN

The second aspect of the challenge is how to keep labor markets open. Under the remarkably liberal provisions of the Treaty of Rome, workers in the existing six member-states were given the right to seek and find work in any member-state. This provision survived the western, southern, and northern enlargements relatively unscathed. Will the same be true of eastern expansion? Public opposition to immigration is vocal in the West. It is possible that the issue of the movement of labor may turn out to be the most problematic of those surrounding enlargement. How serious this problem will become depends upon the pattern of job creation. Where will the jobs be created in the enlarged Europe? Will they be in the CEEC through the stimulus of inward investment and the growth of output? Or will they be in the West, as inflows of labor keep wage rates down and help keep manufacturing sectors competitive? Will the new jobs be in high-skilled occupations, with Western technology married to Eastern education levels and motivation? Or will the jobs be in low-skilled categories, filled by migrant or temporary workers?

Once again, agriculture is at the center of the problem. Agriculture in the ten prospective members will shed labor in the next decade at a rapid rate. The total could approach three million people over the next few years. This would add enormously to pressures on the nonfarm labor market. Where will the displaced workers go? Will they move to cities in the East or jump straight to the labor markets of the West? Movement to the cities in the East will depend upon whether jobs are created in those areas, in turn a function of inward investment and open markets. Can the exodus be stopped by supporting employment in the rural areas? Perhaps for a short time higher support prices might be able to keep people down on the farm, but productivity growth in eastern agriculture will ensure the release of labor regardless of the output prices supported.

GENERATING TRANSFERS

Enlargement of the EU is bound to involve significant transfers from the more to the less developed regions. How to generate these transfers is a key question for policy. Will the transfers come from the budget, through an extension of the regional fund, or from private sources as increased capital investment? If transfers are to be from investment, this is likely only to the extent that the markets are fully open to exports from the new members. If this is not the case, then the transfers will have to be in the form of public funds, as development assistance. The EU is therefore faced with the classic "trade or aid" dilemma. Public transfers would be a heavy but not necessarily intolerable burden for the EU. As current GDP in the ten prospective member countries is only 3 percent of that of the existing EU-15, a transfer equivalent to one-third of their GDP would amount to only 1 percent of the GDP of the EU. As much of this would be spent in the EU, the net cost could be much less.* On the other hand, opening up western markets to eastern goods and investing in new capacity in the East would give a boost to incomes in the West rather than being a burden.

Agriculture represents both a way to generate transfers to the new members and a potential sector for investment of private capital in those countries. The single internal market for agricultural products, presumably still protected against competition from third countries, would again be a sine qua non for such investment. In agriculture the issue of "trade or aid" is usually manifest in a rather direct way. The choice is between high support prices for farmers or income support through targeted payments. The "modern" view is that the use of targeted payments is preferable to high prices. This implies direct fiscal transfers rather than "consumer taxes" built into food prices. However, targeted transfers themselves can achieve different ends. The payments to cereal and oilseed farmers in the EU under the MacSharry reforms were to compensate for price reductions. No one would argue that these payments were to encourage productivity increases or further investment. Indeed the link with set-asides suggests that the transfers are in part an inducement to reduce output. Payments could, however, be given in such a way that farmers used the funds to invest and improve productivity.†

---

*The burden is considerably less, for example, than that of transfers from West to East Germany at the time of unification.

†A parallel would be the PROCAMPO program established in Mexico to convert from high corn prices to funds for productive investment for farmers in the public sector.

ADAPTATION OF CURRENT POLICIES

The Union has a window of perhaps five years to adapt current policies to those which will be appropriate for the more disparate Europe of the future. The two policies which will require most adaptation are the regional and agricultural policies. The regional policy has had to do numerous tasks over the years, from giving the UK some budget payments in the early days of its membership to transferring money to the South to secure the commitment of the Mediterranean countries to the initiatives of the North. The policy will no doubt be able to change yet again to generate transfers to the countries of Central and Eastern Europe.

The CAP has proved more resistant to change. It is implausible that the current CAP will fit a future Union of up to twenty-seven countries. Incorporation of the CEEC into the Union would increase its farming area by 44 percent and its arable area by 55 percent (see Table 1). The issue facing policymakers is not whether to change the CAP but whether to change it in anticipation of enlargement or to wait until pressures build up within the policy which will lead to a collapse of the system.

The normal bureaucratic response to such a dilemma would be to put off action until it is seen as inevitable. However, there is one good reason for not delaying in this case. The CAP changes which would be needed to accommodate the CEEC are themselves desirable. These include the following:

a) Removal of planting requirements to get compensation payments;*
b) Voluntary set-aside, to avoid the situation where some of the best land is idled and poorer quality land stays in production;
c) Extension of lower prices/compensation payments to sugar and dairy and elimination of quotas for these products;
d) Nationalization of the budgetary responsibility for the MacSharry compensation payments over time;

*An interesting parallel is with U.S. farm policy for cereals. Base acreage as well as yields are fixed on an historical basis, and farmers do not have to keep these acres in production just to get compensation payments. The recently discussed Freedom to Farm Act would take this process to its limit by removing any planting constraints as preconditions for payments. The EU policy is evolving toward that used in the United States.

e) Further lowering of market prices so as eventually to remove the need for subsidies and set-asides altogether; and hence ending up with

f) World market prices for the major commodities, decoupled payments in those cases where such compensation is required, and an internationally competitive agriculture for the EU.

GLOBAL DEVELOPMENTS AND THE EXTERNAL MARKET

External developments can also have a significant effect on the process and pace of economic integration. Disparate reactions to external events can split a union in the economic as well as the political realm. A common external commercial policy is sine qua non for a federation and highly desirable as an extension of free internal trade.* Active participation in the global trade system, including the maintenance of open and transparent trade relationships with other regions, is an important part of such an external policy. In the present context this may imply an assumption of leadership of the multilateral trade system, the shiny new WTO, which is at risk at a time when the U.S. Congress seems unlikely to grant the administration any new authority to take initiatives in that area.

Agriculture is again central to these issues. Leadership of the multilateral trade system will require the EU to be more forthcoming in future trade negotiations in agriculture. Such leadership would be compromised by any delay in implementing the Uruguay Round Agreement and its cuts in subsidies. The negotiations scheduled for 1999 to continue the process of trade reform in this area will be a test of the ability of the EU to resist protectionism in favor of openness in agricultural markets. If the CAP is modified along the lines indicated above, the possibility will exist for a more constructive position on agricultural trade liberalization than was taken in the Uruguay Round. If the EU has by the end of the decade a competitive

*It is of course possible to stay at the stage of a free trade area, as EFTA did for years and as NAFTA is likely to do. However, one needs rules of origin to prevent trade deflection, and these rules often open the door to a new form of protectionism. Low, common external tariffs seem to be the only sure way to guarantee no adverse effects from regional integration.

agricultural sector, it will have a strong interest in promoting free trade in other countries.

The transformation of the EU from a reluctant partner in multilateral trade liberalization in agricultural products to a leader in the process will require a consistent strategy. The EU needs to develop an agricultural trade policy for the New Europe to go along with the revamped CAP. This policy would be based on the instruments agreed in the GATT/WTO to be the least trade-distorting and include a modest and relatively uniform level of protection for the major agricultural products. It would avoid the use of sanitary and phytosanitary regulations as instruments of domestic market management and emphasize consumer information and choice rather than central bureaucratic decision.

The emergence of the EU as a champion of the multilateral trade system would bring new challenges. A consistent trade policy would also have to incorporate the approach of the EU to its trading partners and to the development of trade with the regions not currently incorporated into the multilateral trade system. It would need, for instance, to develop a strategy for dealing with Japan and the East Asian countries. Should the EU use bilateral pressure to force open these markets? Or should it tolerate differences in the internal structure of the economies and restrict trade diplomacy to the external policies followed by these countries?

In agriculture these issues are likely to emerge in the next set of WTO talks. The EU could continue to run interference for the protectionist elements in East Asia, taking the brunt of the pressure from the United States and others to liberalize markets. Or the EU itself could put pressure on Asia to open agricultural markets so as to help the export prospects for the newly competitive agriculture of the enlarged EU. This would isolate those governments which have until now resisted international efforts to modify their domestic policies and would almost certainly lead to further trade liberalization.

Equally significant will be the emerging trade relations with the two great countries now outside the mainstream of world commercial rules, China and Russia. How to deal with China and Russia is of course primarily a security issue, with geopolitical overtones which dictate the trade agenda. But the commercial policy aspects of the incorporation of these two giant economies into the WTO system are likely to be of great significance. In the case of Russia, the

EU has an additional decision to make as to how closely to integrate that country into EU markets. A possible free-trade area with Russia has been under discussion for some time, presumably not for realization until the CEEC are safely on board.

In agriculture, these trade relations are likely to be of considerable importance. China has the potential to become a huge import market for agricultural products if it can sell its exports to other countries. Indeed purchases by a rapidly growing China could have an impact on world market prices that would make the reform of the agricultural policy easier. Russia, by contrast, is not likely to offer any new market for EU output of temperate zone agricultural goods in the short to medium term. Indeed Russia is potentially a large supplier of the types of products in ample supply in the EU. The question in the case of Russia is whether to grant that country access to the EU market as a supplier. In economic terms the decision is straightforward: access for Russian goods into the EU market needs to be improved in order to encourage growth and stability in the East. However, from the viewpoint of the politics of an enlarged EU it is not so clear that freer entry of Russian agricultural products would be welcome.

The trade policy for an enlarged EU will need to define anew the relations with developing countries. How should the EU deal with those developing countries that presently enjoy preferential access to the EU market? Should those preferences continue? What will be the impact of the enlargement of the EU on relations with developing countries? It seems highly likely that there will be changes in the Lomé Agreement at its next renewal. The economic value of the agreement to the African-Caribbean-Pacific (ACP) countries will in any case have been reduced by the additional preferences given to other countries and the general reduction in mfn tariffs.

The sugar preferences are safely incorporated in the GATT schedule of the EU but are vulnerable to changes in domestic policy.* If the EU were to reduce domestic support prices, as would happen if serious reform of this market were to be undertaken, then the ACP sugar producers would find that their own support policy had been

---

*The preferential access arrangements for sugar for the U.S. market are also entered into the GATT/WTO schedule.

"reformed." The banana regime is on even more shaky ground, with the possibility of a GATT panel decision or a Court of Justice ruling undermining the legitimacy of the restrictive quota for non-ACP bananas. The preferences have served to maintain export earnings in former colonies and have generally been popular. They have on occasion proved to be a double-edged sword, limiting the development of the overseas producer by locking small countries into a trade pattern with little prospect for growth but too profitable to abandon. The EU needs to rethink its preferential access policy to bring it into line with the current needs of the favored countries as well as with the political realities of the New Europe.

The most pressing task of a trade policy may in fact be to define the relationship with the United States. This issue has recently been revived by a Europe concerned that the United States is drifting into isolationism and/or an obsession with Asia. As a result, there has been considerable discussion on the need for a new transatlantic treaty to keep the United States engaged in Europe. This treaty, by common agreement, would have to have an economic component. What this economic component would be is less clear. Some have argued for a transatlantic free trade area (TAFTA), but governments do not seem to be willing to go this far at present.*

In agriculture the debate on U.S.-EU relations carries with it the fear of failure and frustration, borne of the experience with the Uruguay Round. However, the opportunity should not be lost for an improvement in trade relations in such an important area. Indeed if domestic policy trends continue in both the United States and the EU, there could be an opportunity for dramatic change in trade relations in agriculture in the not too distant future. This could take the form of an agreement to restrict or ban the use of export subsidies, an agreement on domestic policies, and an agreement on SPS standards. However, care will have to be taken to resist the temptation to establish new preferences (unless as a part of a full free-trade area, which would itself only be possible with very low levels of external protection).

*Presumably the enthusiasm for a TAFTA will rise and fall with the prospects of an APEC that achieved trade liberalization within the Asia-Pacific region to the exclusion of Europe. The EU is unlikely to be willing to accept less favored access into the U.S. market than that enjoyed by Japan.

In summary, agricultural domestic and trade policy holds the key to both the enlargement of the EU and European leadership in the multilateral trade system. This link can be either negative—as a brake on progress and a cause of tension—or it can take advantage of a positive connection between a sensible continuation of the reform of the CAP, to adapt it to be able to accommodate the CEEC and push ahead with reform of the agricultural trade system and hence the multilateral trade system as a whole. The rewards are significant enough to make the effort worthwhile.

INSTITUTIONAL CHANGE AND THE AGENDA FOR THE 1996 INTERGOVERNMENTAL CONFERENCE

Francis Jacobs

AGENDA FOR THE 1996 INTERGOVERNMENTAL CONFERENCE: WHAT IS AT STAKE?

The 1996 Intergovernmental Conference (IGC) is not going to produce a big debate on a new European constitution. The most striking development since the last elections to the European Parliament (EP) in 1994 is how dramatically the debate within the Parliament has changed. The word constitution has practically never been mentioned, and when it is mentioned, the response is, "Let's not get bogged down in semantic discussions." Even the word federalism is hardly heard. People seek to avoid language that can provoke an unnecessary debate. Even if the forthcoming IGC does not talk about a new European constitution, however, the question of institutional reform is going to be of central importance. Even to stand still and to defend the existing achievements of the European Union (EU), very important changes need to be made.

The Maastricht Treaty set out a number of formal tasks for the IGC, but these tasks appear much less important than the need to respond to two new challenges that have arisen since the signing of the treaty. The first of these is the need to prepare the EU for its probable further enlargement, especially the need for greater operating efficiency. Second is the need to bring the EU closer to its citizens and to respond, in particular, to the malaise that became apparent during the period of ratification of the Maastricht Treaty. That process revealed the need for a more democratic and transparent EU.

The agenda for the 1996 IGC is thus much less about the need for new EU competences and much more about the functioning of its institutions and procedures. However, it is most likely to be presented in terms of meeting policy objectives, such as increasing internal and external security and fighting unemployment. It will thus attempt to avoid being too overtly "institutional" in order to make the debate more meaningful for the European public and to seek to avoid the negative public response that met the Maastricht Treaty. At the center of the IGC will be how to make the EU institutions and procedures more efficient, transparent, and democratic. Even the policy issues linked to the development of the second and third "pillars" will have important institutional reform components.

There is near consensus on the need for more efficiency, transparency, and democracy. These are noble concepts, but when negotiations begin, there is likely to be less agreement on what each of them means in practice. Moreover, a reconciliation of conflicting criteria will be hard to achieve. The balance between large and small countries, for example, will become a key issue as never before, especially because, compared to the existing members of the EU, many of the potential applicant countries are exceptionally small. In the next wave of enlargement we are going to have Malta and Cyprus. Among the newly created East European states are the Baltic states, Slovakia, and Slovenia. The debate will lead to possible clashes between democracy and efficiency when considering the composition of the institutions.

Here I shall spell out the main issues that are likely to arise at the IGC in these three areas: efficiency, transparency, and democracy.

THE NEED FOR GREATER EFFICIENCY

ISSUES RELATING TO THE FUNCTIONING OF THE COUNCIL OF MINISTERS

A first set of issues to be considered at the IGC is how majority voting can be extended, in which fields unanimity should be retained, and if "reinforced qualified majorities" can be used in certain areas. As the EU expands, unanimous voting in the Council of Ministers becomes increasingly inefficient. When there were only six member-states, unanimity was not nearly so serious as it now is with fifteen. If membership is expanded to twenty-seven or more states, unanimity is clearly a prescription for paralysis. In terms of efficiency the single most important issue is the extent to which majority voting can be further extended. One of the keys will be to look at the matter pragmatically, issue by issue. This is going to be extremely difficult because almost every member-state has a pet area where it wants to retain unanimity. This was shown in the discussions of the "Reflecting Group," a group of personal representatives of the EU member-states that was chaired by the Spaniard Carlos Westendorp and that in the course of 1995 prepared an "annotated agenda" for the IGC. There is more or less a consensus that there are certain critical constitutional-type questions (such as treaty reform and decisions on own resources) where unanimity will need to be retained. In other areas, however, agreement on extending majority voting is going to be much more difficult. The classic example is fiscal harmonization, where a number of member-states will not tolerate a move toward majority voting.

One possible alternative which is being mooted is something between the existing qualified majority voting and unanimity, a kind of super-reinforced majority where the voting threshold needed to obtain approval would be higher than at present—in other words, one that would require the support of most member-states but would prevent one member-state from blocking progress.

A second option will be to "reweight" the votes within the Council. Some people have put forward the concept of double majorities. A favorable vote would require not only a qualified majority of the states but also of populations. This proposal responds to the concern of some bigger member-states, like Germany, which do not think that their population is being adequately reflected in the existing decision-making procedures. This proposal is perhaps less likely to progress than a simpler reweighting of the votes within the Council, whereby the smaller countries would retain the existing number of votes but the larger countries would be given slightly more votes.

A third consideration is the duration of Council presidencies. Some of the big member-states will say that if the EU moves toward twenty-five or more member-states and each gets the presidency for six months or so, it will be twelve and a half years before their presidency comes around. The presidencies will become incoherent, especially on foreign policy questions, and give too much weight to the small member-states. In my view, however, major changes in the status quo are unlikely. The most likely modification to be explored will be a reinforcement of the existing "troika" arrangements among the present, preceding, and following member-states with presidency responsibilities. A less likely but possible version of this would be the creation of a "team presidency," whereby three or even four member-states might share presidency tasks over a longer period.

COMPOSITION OF THE COMMISSION

Again with the objective of efficiency in mind, the IGC will want to consider whether the number of commissioners should be reduced. One or two big member-states, especially France, have been pushing hard for a smaller Commission. Jean-Louis Bourlanges, one of the two rapporteurs of the EP, initially proposed a Commission of six or ten commissioners in the 1995 report on the IGC, but the EP did not follow him in its final resolution and supported the proposal that each member-state should have at least one commissioner. Given the strong objections of a number of member-states, the proposal to reduce the number of commissioners below the number of member-states is unlikely to go far. A possible compromise, however, is for each country to retain a commissioner and at the same time for there to be a reweighting of votes within the Council.

COMPOSITION OF THE EP AND THE EUROPEAN COURTS

Another issue is the composition of the EP itself. Enlargement of the EU poses the thorny issue of how many members large and small countries will be allowed. The EP has already gone from 198 to 626 members. On the present basis an expansion to 27 member-states will produce a parliament of almost a thousand members. Poland alone would have 64 members. Expansion raises the specter of operational gridlock if a limit is not placed on the size of the body. The EP itself has said that 700 is the maximum number of members that it should have in the future. This is going to be an extraordinarily difficult limit to enforce in the face of foreseeable expansion.

In its present unicameral form the EP is trying to reconcile the basis of representation in a senate, with equal representation for each state, and that in a house of representatives, with the number of representatives in the delegation of each state proportional to the state's population. At present in the EP the number of members from each country is based partly on population; thus Germany has ninety-nine members and Luxembourg has only six. But the size of each delegation is not directly proportional to population—there are, for example, 60,000 Luxembourgers for each MEP and 800,000 Germans. The reallocation of seats in the EP within the framework of an overall ceiling to its membership is thus going to be an extremely sensitive issue.

The expansion of the number of members of the EU presents a similar challenge to its judicial branch: the European Court of Justice, the European Court of First Instance, and the European Court of Auditors. Each member-state currently has one of its nationals on each of these bodies. Now the danger is imminent of the courts becoming unwieldy from sheer size, unless the practice is changed. One solution might be for each member-state to have the right to a member on either the Court of Justice or the Court of First Instance or an Advocate General. However, to be acceptable, such an arrangement would have to provide for a real rotation of these posts among countries irrespective of size. A more likely option is a reorganization of the working methods of the courts—for instance, by providing for a structure of separate chambers on which judges of all nationalities within the EU could still be represented.

MORE EFFICIENT DECISION-MAKING PROCEDURES

By one estimate, the EU now employs twenty-two variants of decision-making procedures. There is an evident need to simplify this process in the name of efficiency, if for no other reason. As far as decision-making procedures are concerned, the EP has pushed hard to reduce the procedures in which it is involved to three: consultation, EP/Council co-decision, and assent (whereby the EP has the right to say yes or no but not to make amendments). The existing cooperation procedure should be eliminated and co-decision should apply to all legislation. A second possible change is to simplify the co-decision procedure. In practice it has worked reasonably well, but the existing procedure is still complicated, and there are some ways in which it could be streamlined.

GREATER EFFICIENCY IN THE PREDOMINANTLY INTERGOVERNMENTAL FIELDS OF COMMON FOREIGN AND SECURITY POLICY AND HOME AFFAIRS AND JUSTICE

A further set of efficiency-related issues concerns decision-making procedures in the so-called second and third "pillars," dealing respectively with foreign and security policy and with home affairs and justice. At present they are exceedingly inefficient in their operation. The field of justice and home affairs, for example, currently has a five-tier decision-making structure, while foreign and security policy lacks a single common analytical capacity. One solution for which the EP has pushed (and which is unfortunately unlikely to occur) is to merge these two pillars with the first or "community" pillar. Even if the separate pillars are retained, however (either totally or partially), their workings could be made much more effective than at present. As the discussions in the Reflection Group showed, a large majority of member-states agree that this needs to be done.

USE OF LANGUAGES IN THE EU

This is a classic issue of the balance among efficiency, transparency, and democracy in that the criterion of efficiency would call for future restrictions in the number of EU languages, whereas the criteria of transparency and democracy call for every citizen to be able to read an EU text or to express himself/herself in his/her own language. In the case of conflict, the EP has called for the latter criteria to prevail since the EU is not a classic intergovernmental organization run by diplomats. The scope for reducing EU languages, while desirable on efficiency grounds, is thus very limited.

THE NEED FOR GREATER TRANSPARENCY

Increasing transparency in the running of the EU involves two main components. One calls for the EU to be more open in its functioning, the other for the processes of the EU to be more comprehensible to its citizens.

OPENNESS

One reform that is likely to be made at the IGC is for a treaty provision to be adopted declaring "openness" to be an explicit objective of the EU. While partially symbolic, it would also give practical weight to subsequent measures to implement the concept of openness within EU institutions and to reduce the present unacceptable level of secrecy.

One recommendation made by the EP is to open up meetings of the Council to the public when the Council is acting in its legislative capacity. This is a highly desirable objective, but I am skeptical as to how much real progress is possible. People will say that this reform is artificial because if all legislative meetings of the Council are public, negotiations will just take place in another informal setting. For example, certain big debates (such as the ECOFIN meetings of the Finance Minister) are at the moment televised, but having on one occasion gone along to see how it worked, I can report that it was a complete farce. I was put in a room watching closed-circuit television with two journalists and one other member of the public. We watched ministers reading prepared statements for about two hours, and then the closed-circuit television coverage closed down, and the ministers got down to a real debate.

A means of implementing openness that might be less difficult to achieve would be for documents emanating from EU bodies to be made more readily available to the public. The Swedes and the Finns in particular are pressing to ensure public access to EU documentation. The possibility of improvement in this area has been reinforced by the legal victory of the *Guardian* in the recent case against the Council concerning the disclosure of documents. The judgment is of limited scope, but it leaves the door open for more progress toward greater public access to documents. The Swedes have pointed out that one of the weaknesses of the present system is the lack of proper guidelines as to what documentation should be confidential. One of the advantages of a system of openness is a much tighter definition of which type of information needs to be confidential and which should be freely disclosed.

A MORE COMPREHENSIBLE EU

Another aspect of transparency is to establish a more comprehensible EU. Citizens of the EU, who have to deal with their own national and local governments, become understandably baffled when they are faced with a new set of institutions, codes, and practices, especially since these do not always jibe with the bodies and rules they are used to. If the EU is to be a welcome addition to their lives, they must understand its workings and appreciate its objectives. There is currently a lack of transparency arising from complexity. Clearer and simpler EU structures and procedures, which are needed for efficiency, are thus also important in this context.

A big effort is going to be made to produce a simplified treaty. The Council legal service has just finished a very interesting study complementing one already carried out for the EP that shows how, without actually changing the content of the existing treaties, many redundant articles can be eliminated, and how the different treaties can be restructured into something more readable and comprehensible. One can start, for instance, by grouping together fundamental and other rights at the beginning of the treaty. If the content of the treaties could be changed, even more progress could be made—for example, by abolishing the present pillar structure and the existing European Coal and Steel Community and EURATOM treaties and grouping them together within a single consolidated treaty framework. However far this exercise goes, and even if the debate over a European constitution is not being revived, it can thus be recognized that the EU already has a kind of rough and ready constitutional framework but that there is considerable scope for it to be restructured, strengthened, and simplified.

THE NEED FOR GREATER DEMOCRACY

The final topic is the need for greater democracy. This also has two main components—first, the issue of whether the EP and the different national parliaments should be given more power, and second, issues related to the rights of EU citizens and of all those resident in the EU.

POWERS OF THE EP

As regards the powers of the EP, three main sets of issues are likely to be posed. The first is an extension of EP/Council co-decision in legislative and budgetary areas. The EP would like co-decision to be extended to all legislation but at least to all areas where the Council decides by qualified majority voting. A more likely outcome is that it will be extended to areas currently covered by the cooperation procedure, but preliminary discussion in the Reflection Group has tended to focus on extension on a case-by-case basis. It thus appears unlikely that the EP's demands will be met in full; nevertheless, most member-states appear to support at least some extension of the co-decision procedure.

At the moment the EP has considerable budgetary powers, but it is hamstrung by the fact that in certain categories of expenditure it does not have the same powers. It would like this situation to be reformed by an extension of budgetary co-decision. It would like to eliminate the current distinction between obligatory and nonobligatory expenditure, and it wants to be involved on the revenue as well as the expenditure side of the budget. There was unfortunately little support for these demands within the Reflection Group.

A second extension of the powers of the EP applies to its involvement in nomination to top EU posts. One of the innovations of the Maastricht Treaty was to give the EP a new role in the investiture of the Commission, first in approving the choice of the Commission president and then of the Commission as a whole. Should this procedure, which was used for the first time in 1994, be further modified by giving the EP more power—for example, by permitting it to elect the president of the Commission or to have more of a say over the choice (and possible subsequent firing) of individual commissioners? The latter issue poses a very important question about the continuance of collective responsibility of the Commission.

In other areas of nomination, such as the European Monetary Institute and the European Central Bank, the existing role of the EP is simply to be consulted. Should the role be extended to giving advice and consent—that is, to being able to veto a nomination? This issue is also posed as regards nominations to the European Court of Auditors, where at the moment the EP is restricted to providing nonbinding consultation. On a couple of occasions on which the EP has said "no" to a nominee, the Council has ignored it. Should its assent be required here too? The same question arises with judicial nominations. Should the EP have to give its assent, or at least be consulted, for appointments to the European Court of Justice, Advocates General, and the European Court of First Instance?

Finally, should the EP's role be extended in other fields where it is currently weak, such as foreign and security policy, home affairs and justice, or economic and monetary union? The EP is not arguing for co-decision in these fields, but it is pushing at least for greatly increased information and consultation rights.

REINFORCED ROLE FOR THE NATIONAL PARLIAMENTS ON EU MATTERS

The role of national parliaments on EU matters is also a critical issue. It immediately raises the controversial question of a new second European chamber or senate of delegated national parliamentarians, an idea put forward by the French. It is very interesting that no other national parliament sided explicitly with the French in favor of such a second chamber. This was for a variety of reasons, but many felt that a second chamber would be a cumbersome and awkward body and would go against the very simplification which I discussed above. A second chamber would make the EU's structure even more complicated and unmanageable, and national parliamentarians would not have the time anyway.

There is, however, general agreement on the need to strengthen the role of national parliaments, and there are a number of other ways in which this could be done. One possibility is to give national parliaments the right to go to the European Court of Justice on subsidiarity or other grounds. Some strongly oppose this proposal, but it is likely to be raised at the IGC. A second possibility is for the existing declaration on the role of national parliaments, which accompanied the Maastricht Treaty, to be included directly within the treaty. A third and related proposal that would reinforce the rights of national parliaments in scrutinizing EU legislation would be to provide that the Council could not take a decision on legislation until the national parliaments had had a minimum period of time (for instance, a month or six weeks) to consider it, except in certain urgent cases. Another possibility is for national parliaments to comment on the annual EU legislative program, which is currently agreed between the EP and the Commission.

The most likely change lies in reinforced coordination between the EP and national parliaments. This will probably not take the form of "assises" or a big meeting of national parliaments and the EP. This took place once before the Maastricht Treaty. The EP was quite satisfied with it, but the national parliaments were not. The national parliaments would generally prefer to develop what in EU jargon is called the COSAC. This consists of meetings between a small delegation from the EP and European Communities Committees of all the different national parliaments. It meets at the moment twice a year and is less cumbersome than the much larger-scale "assises." There seems to be a rather broad agreement that the scope could be further extended, perhaps by having specialized meetings on particular subjects, since it provides a rather flexible form of cooperation among national parliaments themselves and also with the EP.

Reinforced cooperation between the individual specialized committees of the national parliaments and the EP is yet another and perhaps even more useful route. Underlying any such changes, however, is the need to define more carefully the objectives of such cooperation and to undertake a case-by-case analysis of the extent of democratic accountability that currently exists in the different areas of the EU, such as in the third pillar, for instance, or the European Monetary Union (EMU). Such a review would provide a better idea of which areas are currently not subject to adequate democratic scrutiny by either the EP or national parliaments and where there thus needs to be better control of the "executive" (the Council, the Commission, and national administrations acting in the EU capacity).

RIGHTS OF CITIZENS

Finally, can the content of EU citizenship be further strengthened, and if so how? For lack of space, I shall not go into this critical topic. I am pessimistic about the meaningful progress that is likely to be made in this area, but at least it will be on the IGC agenda, and there are useful ideas as to how the rights of EU citizens may be strengthened. In addition, the position of non-EU citizens who are resident in the EU (especially those who are residing on a long-term basis) may also be reinforced.

FINAL REMARKS

The above are just some of the institutional issues which are likely to be raised at the IGC in the context of increasing efficiency, transparency, and democracy. If satisfactory solutions are found to these issues, the EU can evolve in a way which will make it both closer to its citizens and better adapted for its further enlargement.

INTERNATIONAL AND AREA STUDIES

University of California at Berkeley

Richard M. Buxbaum, Dean

2223 Fulton Street, 3d floor Berkeley, California 94720

Recent books published by International and Area Studies:

RESEARCH SERIES

83. *The Contradictory Alliance: State-Labor Relations and Regime Change in Mexico.* Ruth Berins Collier. $18.50
84. *The Future of European Security.* Ed. Beverly Crawford. $23.50
85. *High Technology and Third World Industrialization: Brazilian Computer Policy in Comparative Perspective.* Eds. Peter B. Evans, Claudio R. Frischtak, & Paulo Bastos Tigre. $14.95
86. *The New Portugal: Democracy and Europe.* Ed. Richard Herr. $15.50
87. *Russia and Japan: An Unresolved Dilemma between Distant Neighbors.* Eds. T. Hasegawa, J. Haslam, and A. Kuchins. $26.50
88. *Political Parties in Russia.* Ed. Alexander Dallin. $10.95
89. *European Dilemmas after Maastricht.* Eds. Beverly Crawford and Peter W. Schulze. $22.95
90. *The Soldiers' Story.* Anna Heinämaa, Maija Leppänen, and Yuri Yurchenko, eds. $12.50
91. *Deconstructing Italy: Italy in the Nineties.* Ed. Salvatore Sechi. $23.50
92. *Ivo Andrić Revisited: The Bridge Still Stands.* Ed. Wayne S. Vucinich. $18.95

EXPLORATORY ESSAYS

1. *The Question of Food Security in Cuban Socialism.* Laura J. Enríquez. $7.50
2. *The Collapse of Soviet Communism: A View from the Information Society.* Manuel Castells and Emma Kiselyova $9.50

INSTITUTE OF INTERNATIONAL STUDIES

POLICY PAPERS IN INTERNATIONAL AFFAIRS

39. *Lessons of the Gulf War: Ascendant Technology and Declining Capability.* Gene I. Rochlin and Chris C. Demchak. $5.50
40. *Impediments on Environmental Policy-Making and Implementation in Central and Eastern Europe: Tabula Rasa vs. Legacy of the Past.* Peter Hardi. $6.50
41. *Flying Apart? Japanese-American Negotiations over the FSX Fighter Plane.* Gregory W. Noble. $7.25
42. *Beware the Slippery Slope: Notes Toward the Definition of Justifiable Intervention.* Ernst B. Haas. $6.50
43. *Industrial Policy Supporting Economic Transition in Central-Eastern Europe: Lessons from Slovenia.* Tea Petrin $6.95

INSIGHTS IN INTERNATIONAL AFFAIRS

1. *Confrontation in the Gulf: University of California Professors Talk about the War.* Ed. Harry Kreisler. $7.95

2. *Refugees: A Multilateral Response to Humanitarian Crises.*
   Sadako Ogata. $5.95
3. *American Intervention after the Cold War.* Robert W. Tucker. $3.95
4. *Crisis in the Balkans.* Eugene A. Hammel, Irwin M. Wall,
   and Benjamin N. Ward. $6.95

CENTERS FOR SOUTH AND SOUTHEAST ASIA STUDIES
MONOGRAPH SERIES

32. *Scavengers, Recyclers, & Solutions for Solid Waste Management in Indonesia.* Daniel T. Sicular. $16.50
33. *Indonesian Transmigrants and Adaptation: An Ecological Anthropological Perspective.* Oekan S. Abdoellah. $14.95
34. *Thai Music and Musicians in Contemporary Bangkok.* Pamela Myers-Moro. $22.50
35. *In the Shadow of Change: Images of Women in Indonesian Literature.* Tineke Hellwig. $22.00

OCCASIONAL PAPERS

15. *The Penis Inserts of Southeast Asia: An Annotated Bibliography with an Overview & Comparative Perspective.* Donald E. Brown, J. W. Edwards, & R. P. Moore. $6.00
16. *Patterns of Migration in Southeast Asia.* Ed. Robert R. Reed. $19.50
17. *Bridging Worlds: Studies on Women in South Asia.* Ed. Sally J. M. Sutherland. $17.50
18. *Essays on Southeast Asian Performing Arts: Local Manifestations and Cross-Cultural Implications.* Ed. Kathy Foley. $14.95

LANGUAGE TEACHING MATERIALS

Introduction to Hindi Grammar. Usha Jain. $30.00

Hmong for Beginners. Annie Jaisser et al. $28.00

Devavanipravesika: Introduction to the Sanskrit Language. Robert P. Goldman and Sally J. Sutherland. $23.50

Teaching Grammar of Thai. William Kuo. $23.50

Tamil for Beginners, 2 vols. Kausalya Hart. $12.50 ea.

SINO-TIBETAN ETYMOLOGICAL DICTIONARY AND THESAURUS PROJECT
MONOGRAPH SERIES

1A. *Bibliography of the International Conferences on Sino-Tibetan Languages and Linguistics I-XXV*, 2d ed. Randy J. LaPolla and John B. Lowe $28.00